CW01631152

Sports Action

Squash

Edited by
Richard Eaton

OCTOPUS BOOKS

Acknowledgements
Photographs
Cover picture: Russell Cheyne/Allsport
D. Birkner 6, 8, 9, 10 right, 11 right, 14, 15, 16, 17, 21, 29, 43 upper, 50, 51, 61, 63, 65, 67, 69, 70, 71, 72, 74, 75, 76, 78, 85, 101, 102, 116; Dunlop archive 119; R. Espie 32; J. Kemmier 18-9, 20, 22-3, 24, 25, 26-7, 28, 30-1, 34-5, 36, 37, 38, 39, 40, 41, 42(3, 44-5, 46, 49-9, 56-7, 58-9, 60-1; W. Krecichwest 33 top left, 47; K. Wiese 10 left, 11 left

Published in 1989 by
Octopus Books Limited
Michelin House
81 Fulham Road
London SW3 6RB

English Translation
© 1989 Octopus Books Limited

Title of original German edition
Richtig Squash
by Robin Espie and Martin Sklorz
© 1982 BLV Verlagsgesellschaft mbH, Munich

ISBN 0 7064 5005 1

Photoset by
SX Composing Limited
Rayleigh, Essex
Produced by Mandarin Offset
Printed and bound in Hong Kong

Contents

Foreword

This book aims to help make it easier for anyone interested to learn to play the game quickly and well.

It is structured in such a way that it can be used as a manual by both casual and dedicated players alike without any problem. We have laid particular value on a clear and lucid presentation of theory, technique, tactics and training.

Club coaches, games teachers at school, trainers in leisure, work-place and fitness groups now have a clear, systematic instruction handbook. We wish all interested parties lots of fun while learning and, especially, when playing.

Robin Espie
Martin Sklorz

Introduction

Who can play squash? – Anybody!

Squash is the only racket sport that is played with different balls, suitable for every level of player: a bouncy one for beginners, a rather slower one for more advanced players, and a sluggish one for experts.

This means that anyone with any degree of interest can reasonably take up the game. Moreover, squash is the easiest racket sport to learn. Anyone can play a match after only two hours or so.

Whether you are young or old, male or female: anyone can partake in this sport with, or against, anyone else.

Where do you play squash? – On a court.

This sport can only be played on a special court, but for practising individual strokes you can use any interior or exterior wall or vertical surface in your training.

Practise stroke techniques at home and make use of what opportunities you have. Beginners in particular can acquire the basic techniques both quickly and soundly this way.

Playing on a court is then even more fun.

What does squash teach you? – All sorts!

It gives intensive training in:

Physical abilities

- Stamina
- Speed
- Strength
- Agility
- Co-ordination

Personal qualities

- Concentration
- Reactions
- Self-control
- Critical faculties

But also

- Conviviality
- Fair play.

What is the risk of injury from squash? – Small.

This may come as a surprise to many people but it is true for anyone who:

- has a sensible warm-up before training or before a match
- has thoroughly mastered the rules
- has had proper technical and tactical guidance from a coach.

Such players run scarcely any risk of injuring either themselves or other players.

Experience and statistics demonstrate that injuries and accidents happen when people play for fun without any of these precautions.

How many places offer squash? – Lots.

As interest in squash has grown and its value has been recognised, squash can be played in

- sports clubs
- schools
- colleges
- leisure centres
- hotels.

Go along to a squash club; they have practice sessions for recreational players who don't want to take part in competitions.

Is squash expensive? – No!

To be a well-equipped casual player will cost you:

- Racket = £20-£40
- Ball = £1.50

You don't need any special clothing.

Clubs make the following annual membership charges:

- Adults = £100 – £300
- Children = £80 upwards

Rental for a court is £1.50 to £2.00 for 45 minutes at off-peak times, and up to twice as much after 5 pm.

Almost all squash clubs charge differently depending on the time of day. They are cheapest before and during the afternoon.

Will you learn squash quicker with a coach? – Yes!

There is no question about this. To get the most out of this fantastic sport you should definitely learn with a trainer. If no coach is available you will have to find someone to play with, so you can help and discuss each other's game.

Important Every bit of information and every little tip will help your partner.

Praise but never reproach your partners.

You will also learn faster if you master the basics of theory (see the chapter on theory), so a squash book as a guide will be an advantage to you.

When can you play squash? – Anytime!

There is no squash season and you should make the most of this enormous advantage. Regardless of where you play squash you should do so regularly; training several times a week is ideal.

A few tips:

- Warm up before playing
- Take a short break after 15 minutes
- Play with different partners
- Play hard
- Analyse faults quickly – keep calm

Golden Rules

To learn all stroke techniques quickly and surely you should always follow these principles:

Ten golden rules for playing squash well

1. Check that you are using the right grip and holding the racket properly.
2. Position your feet and body properly for shots.
3. Keep a good distance between your body and the ball.
4. Play vigorously; your whole body should be in motion.
5. Perform strokes cleanly.
6. Always angle your racket arm during the backswing.
7. Control your racket arm during the follow-through with no rotational swing.
8. Emphasise individual phases of the stroke action (backswing, impact or follow-through) in case faults occur during these phases.
9. Run through a stroke technique after a bad shot, trying the correct action without a ball.
10. Practise techniques mentally: play the shot through in your mind without actually carrying out the actions.

Learning Method

Squash, like any other sport or subject, should be learnt and taught systematically, by means of instruction, practice, discussion, assessment and revision.

Ten golden rules for learning squash

1. If at all possible, practise with a trainer (but remember, a partner can give you valuable tips too).
2. Perform the strokes in a systematic, disciplined and determined way.
3. Practise the simple strokes first (basic techniques) and then the more complicated ones (special techniques).
4. Safe and precise shots are more important than hard ones.
5. Analyse mistakes and then correct them.
6. Don't get disappointed if you can't see any great progress in your learning – that is a normal part of the learning process.
7. You will learn more quickly if you understand the theoretical principles of a stroke.
8. Only praise your partner – negative criticism is a mistake.
9. Halve your squash lesson strictly: spend half on training exercises and half on match play exercises.
10. Playing squash should be fun and if it isn't you won't make much progress in your learning.

Basic techniques

Player and coach – a team.

The great advantage of squash – compared with other games – is that it can be learnt quickly. Many beginners can play the game within a short time, even without any instruction. This can also be a great danger, however.

Usually, beginners will simply carry on playing without ever considering whether their play is technically correct. After a short time they will sadly realise that their game isn't improving. They make the same mistakes again and again and can only control the ball in simple situations. No matter how hard they try they just don't get any better, which leads to frustration and resignation.

This problem can be avoided if you learn the right way to do things from the start. To begin with, you must practise the elementary techniques, of which the most basic are the right grip on the racket and the proper positions and stances for the different shots. These will give you a sound foundation on which to learn more advanced strokes, making your game more varied and so more fun.

- Learn the correct technique from the start.
- Find yourself a coach or trainer, who will give you the specialist guidance you need for fast, successful learning.
- Don't give up if everything doesn't go right first time. Everybody has had difficulties learning a technique at some time or other.
- Praise your partner during training.
- Play in a concentrated and systematic way.
- Always stay on the move during rallies.
- Never play if you really don't feel like it.

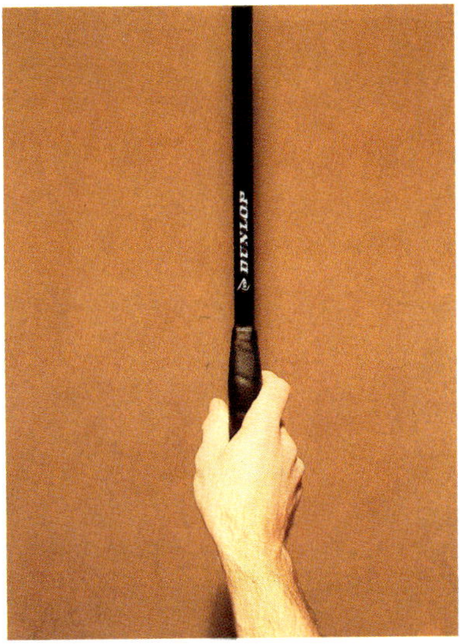

Correct grip – the basis of all techniques

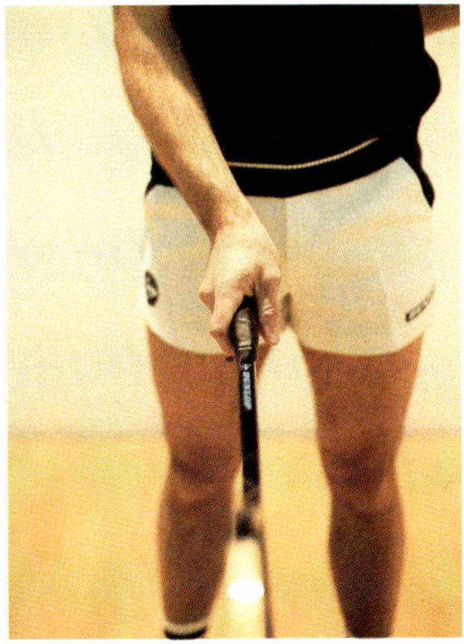

V grip

Basics

Grip

Important All instructions are for right-handers.

All strokes depend on the right grip for perfect execution. This means that it's particularly important for beginners to pay special attention to ensuring they always hold the racket properly. Having a poor grip is the worst mistake any squash player can make and should be avoided from the start.

Grip

- Hold the racket out in front of you in your left hand with the racket face perpendicular to the floor and the grip towards you.
- Form a V shape with the thumb and forefinger of your right hand.
- Take the grip in your right hand. The centre of the V should be over the left edge of the grip.

Important The forefinger lies in front of the thumb and the fingers are slightly splayed.

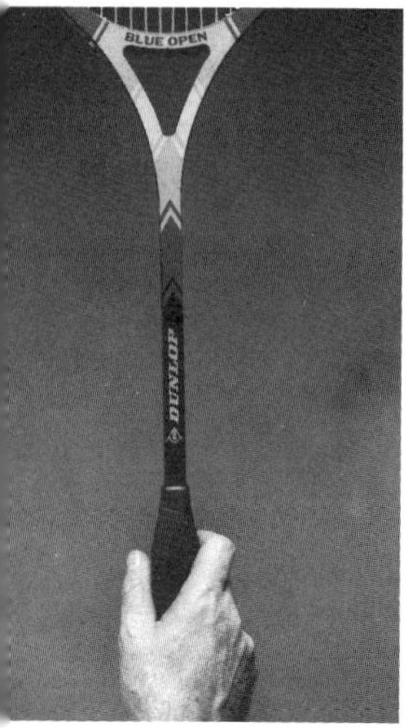

Wrong – racket face horizontal

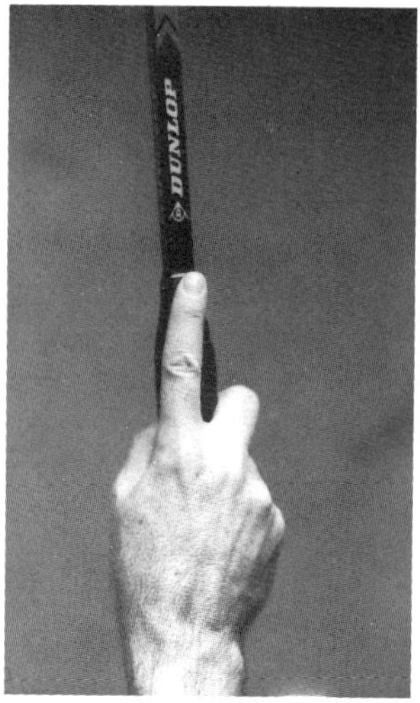

Wrong – forefinger lying along handle

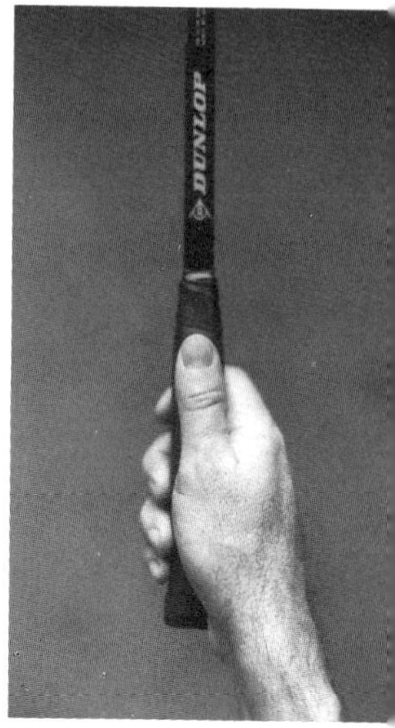

Wrong – thumb lying along handle

Tips for a correct grip

- Get used to the grip by turning the racket in your hand until you find the V grip blind.
- Don't hold the handle too tightly.
- The racket head should always be pointing upwards. Never angle your wrist downwards.
- The end of the handle should touch the heel of your hand. Some slight individual variations are possible, such as
  - the end of the handle may rest just within the palm
  - the end of the handle may extend slightly beyond the palm.

Correct Grip

Ready position

Squash is an exceptionally fast game. To be able to play good sound shots in the short reaction time available you must take up a precise ready position. Your body needs to be on stand-by to allow you to move off immediately in **any direction** with equal ease.

Features

- Ankles, knees and hips are all slightly bent.
- Feet are shoulder width apart.
- Weight is evenly distributed on the balls of the feet.
- The racket hand is in front of the body (somewhere between hip and chest height).
- The racket arm is bent.
- The racket head is raised (somewhere between chest and head height).
- Eyes are on the ball.

When you are in the ready position your whole body should be in a concentrated but not tense state. Only in this way will you be at your best for any action.

Ready positions
Above: from the front
Below: from the side

1

2

3

Forehand drive

Both technically and tactically, the forehand and backhand drives are the most important squash strokes for beginners and experts alike.

All shots can be divided into three phases

- backswing
- impact
- follow-through

Forehand drive technique

Backswing

The backswing must be kept compact and must be played early. Important features are to

- Take up the ready position early.
- Take the racket back to the right, which will make your upper body turn right, too.
- Bend your racket arm at the elbow at about a right angle.
- Bend your hand back at the wrist.
- Point your racket head upwards and well behind you.

Typical backswing faults

- Too late – the shot is hectic.
- Arm stretched out – backswing too wide and slow.
- Hand bent inwards – closed racket face, ball goes into the tin.

4

5

6

Body position at impact

- Stand sideways on to the ball.
- Lunge forwards on the left foot.
- Keep your feet wide apart.
- Assume a bent position.
- Shift your weight on to the left leg.
- Look forwards.
- Arch your back.

Distance from ball at impact

- Keep a good distance between you and the ball.
- Strike the ball in front of your left foot.

Important Under no circumstances get too close to the ball! If you do it will be impossible to play a correct and technically perfect shot. Errors will be inevitable.

Always try to keep well away from the ball and take a large lunge. If you keep the right distance from the ball it will be easier to achieve a good body position. Your ball control and hitting power will improve immediately.

Stroke action

- Let your racket arm travel through as if you were skimming a pebble over water.
- Keep your arm flexed and your hand turned back until just before impact so that the racket face stays slightly open.
- Give the ball a little bottom slice on the swing.
- During the impact phase flick your wrist forwards.

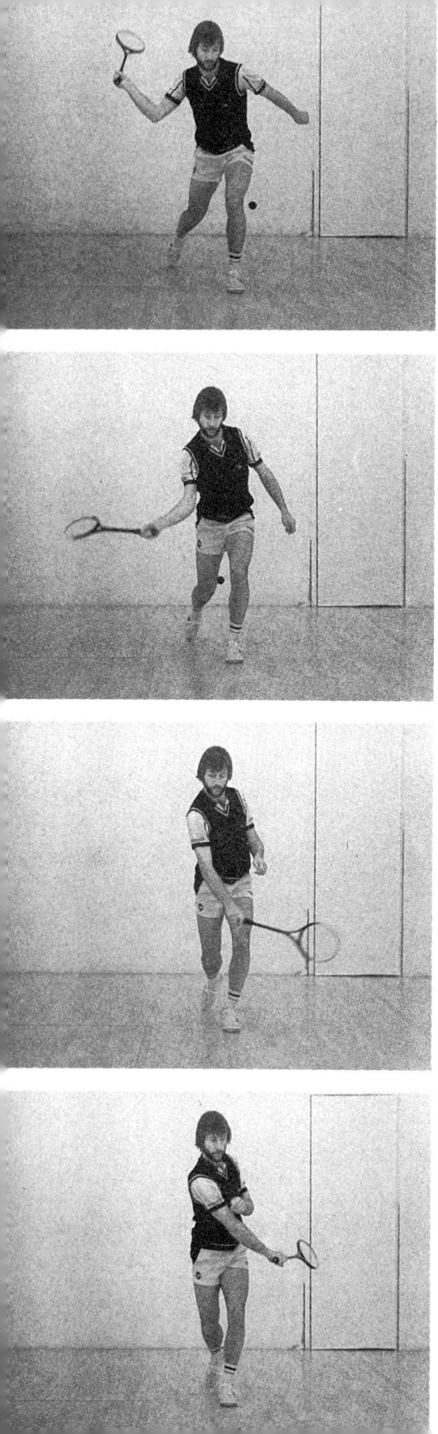

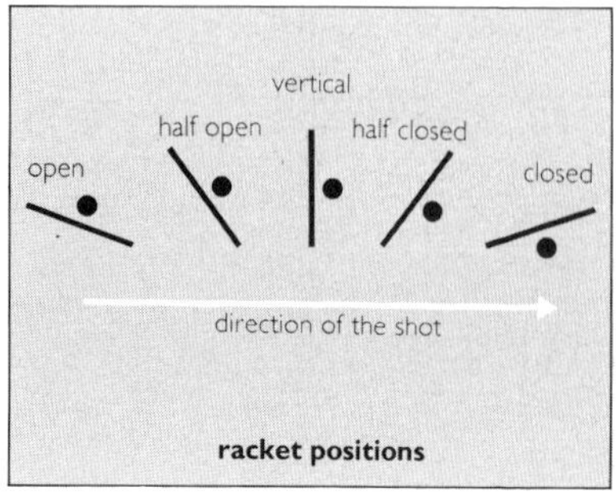

racket positions

Follow-through

- Take your racket a short way through in the direction of the stroke.
- The stroke action ends with a follow-through towards your left shoulder.

Important Make sure you don't overdo the follow-through or

- the excessive shift of weight will upset your balance.
- you may hit your opponent.

Crosscourt drive

In this shot the ball is played diagonally, not parallel. The stroke technique is the same but the ball is taken a little earlier and you should face the front wall a little more.

Left: The crosscourt drive

Right: Follow-through of the forehand drive

SPALDING

1

2

3

Backhand drive

Many beginners dread the backhand. Top players, however, prefer this side and use it to produce greater speed and accuracy on the ball than the forehand does, and with less exertion too.

The position of your right shoulder is different on the backhand drive from on the forehand drive. For this reason, the backhand shot should be accompanied by a twist of your upper body. Initial problems with the backhand are usually a result of players only using their arm or wrist on the shot, and not their shoulders and upper body.

Technique

Backswing

- Take up the readiness position with your hand and elbow correctly positioned as for the forehand.
- Begin the stroke action early.
- Take the racket back to the left; at the same time bringing your right shoulder around forwards and left to about below your chin.
- Flex your racket arm at the elbow.
- Raise your racket hand to about shoulder height.
- Turn your hip emphatically to the left.

Important Take care that your shoulder and not just your arm is brought around as clearly illustrated in picture 3 above.

4

5

6

Body position

This is the position as on the forehand, only reversed.

- Lunge on the right leg.

Distance from ball at impact

- Hit the ball in front of your body. If the ball is taken too late you lose all the advantages of the backhand drive.

Stroke action

- Move your right shoulder and hip very quickly forwards.
- Drop your hand and elbow. Your racket arm is pulled by your shoulder, i.e. the shoulder movement precedes the arm movement.
- Reach out with your racket arm to the ball.
- Turn your forearm slightly inwards to open the racket face.

Follow-through

- Swing your arm out over your right shoulder.
- The follow-through must be kept short and controlled.

Typical backhand faults

- Backswing too late – shot is hectic and can no longer be played with technical perfection.
- Elbows too high during backswing – no ball control.
- No shoulder turn on the stroke – no unleashing of power.
- Follow-through too expansive – partner endangered.

Volley

The volley is indispensable if you want to add tactical pressure to your game. Without a good volley you will find it difficult to control the centre of the court, the T. First, you must master the long volley, which should make the ball fly well to the back of the court. All other types of volley are dealt with in the chapter on special techniques.

Technique

The technique is similar to that for the drive, the differences being:
The ball is hit higher
You have less time to make the shot, so it is played a little faster
The stroke action is shorter

Backswing

- Swing back early.
- Make the backswing short.

Impact

- The action is as for a drive.
- Shift your weight as on the drive.
- Shorten the action slightly.
- Keep the racket face open.
- The impact point should be in front of your body.

Follow-through

Follow-through is short.

Left: Forehand volley

Right: Backhand volley

1

2

3

4

1

2

3

Rear court techniques

Most players have their greatest difficulties with balls between the side and rear walls. The main problem in these cases is the narrowness of the space. The side and rear walls prevent you playing a tidy shot. Also, there is little time to play it.

It is tactically disadvantageous to be in a rear corner. The best means of defence is a longline shot.
You must take up the right rear corner stance at the walls, otherwise you won't be able to play the ball properly.

Important Don't attempt to hit the ball hard from a rear corner position, there isn't enough room. Try to play the ball gently and high on to the front wall.

45° straight technique

The 45° straight technique is very important for a technically sound return. It means that your body must be at a 45° angle to the rear wall to play a straight ball without the racket hitting the rear wall.

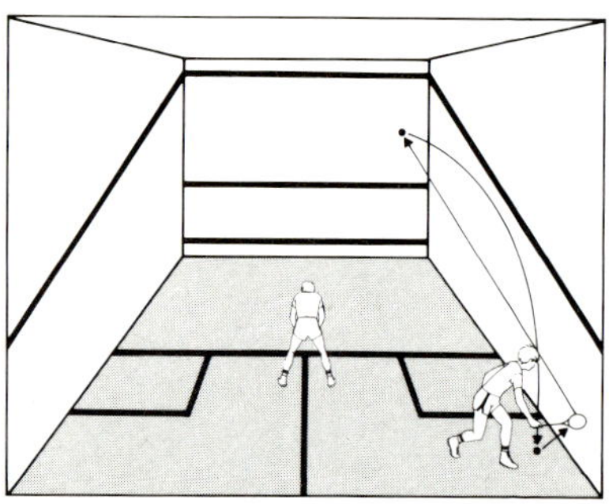

Forehand in rear corner

- Turn your body. Face the rear corner with your back to the front wall.
- With a short backswing take the racket back early.

4

5

6

- Stand with your left foot at 45° to the rear wall.
- Lunge.
- Put your left foot down near the rear wall.
- Crouch right down, with your weight on your left leg, back arched and feet apart.

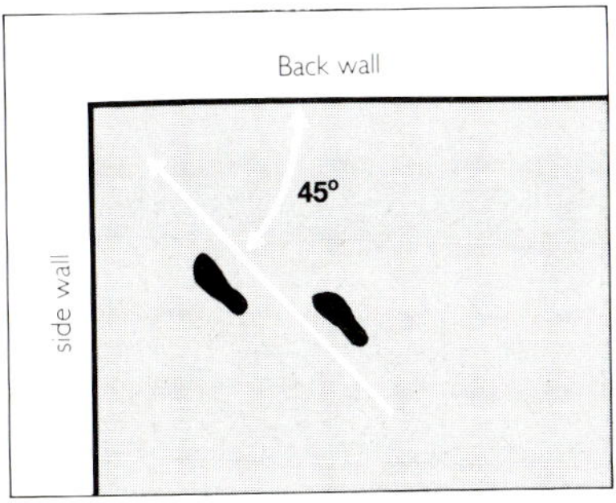

45° position

- Wait until the ball bounces off the back wall and comes down in front of your left foot. Don't rush onto it.
- Make a shortened stroke action (as for a volley), keeping your elbow close to your body.

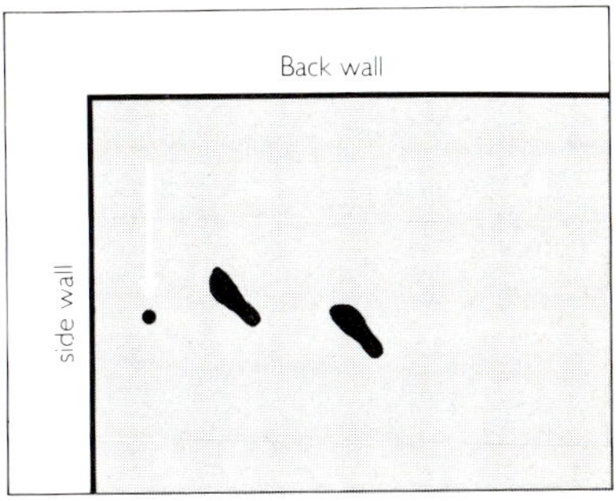

Impact on ball using 45° technique

- Play the ball high onto the front wall with an open racket face.

Important if you are at a true 45° angle the racket won't touch the wall. The longline shot can only be played if you are close to the rear wall and limit your stroke action. Expansive stroke actions always lead to the racket hitting the wall and mistakes being made.

Backhand in rear corner

The same technique applies to the backhand as to the forehand, with the position of your body and feet reversed.

- The correct relationship of feet to ball is an indispensable feature of the 45° technique.
- Put your foot down near the rear wall.
- Don't hit the ball too early, but wait until it bounces off the rear wall.

Correcting faults

- Ball played too hard and inaccurately.
  Hit more gently.
- Racket touching rear wall during stroke action.
  Stand at 45°.
- Return not longline but always played as boast.
  Learn the 45° technique.
- Racket hitting side wall when playing shot.
  Keep your distance from the side wall.

Using the corners

Squash becomes real fun only when you have mastered the rear corner techniques. Practise them systematically and in every training session and you will learn to use them successfully.

Right: Backswing on forehand, 45° technique

1

2

3

Rear corner defensive boast

There are shots that can't be returned using the 45° technique because your opponent has played a precise shot that bounces only a short way off the back wall. A straight drive from this position will generally lead to an error.

In this situation you should play only a defensive boast, the boast being a shot that is played off the side wall onto the front wall.

On a defensive boast the ball first travels high and slow to the side wall and then onto the front wall. The ball isn't slammed but played onto the wall using an upward-scooping action.

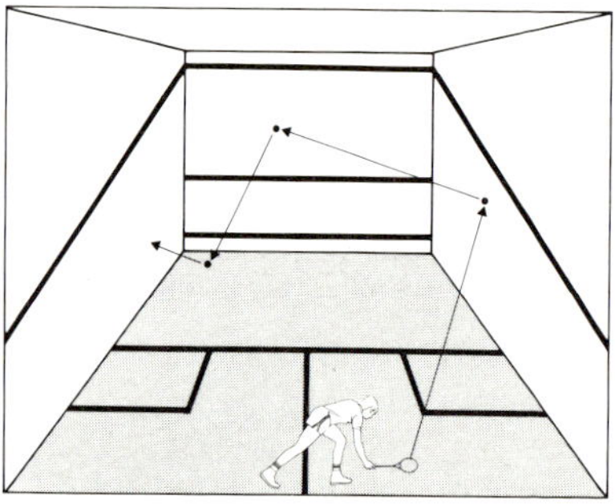

Ball's path on back corner defensive boast

4

5

6

Technique

- Stand as close to the rear wall as possible.
- Take a shortened backswing.
- Crouch right down.
- Take the racket head under the ball and lift the ball using your wrist and forearm.
- Lift the ball high up onto the side wall. The ball should hit the side wall well to the front towards the front wall.
- Run quickly to the T.

Important Use a lifting rather than a striking motion. You will probably hit the rear wall if you play a normal stroke and so mishit the ball. Stand close to the wall in the right stance.

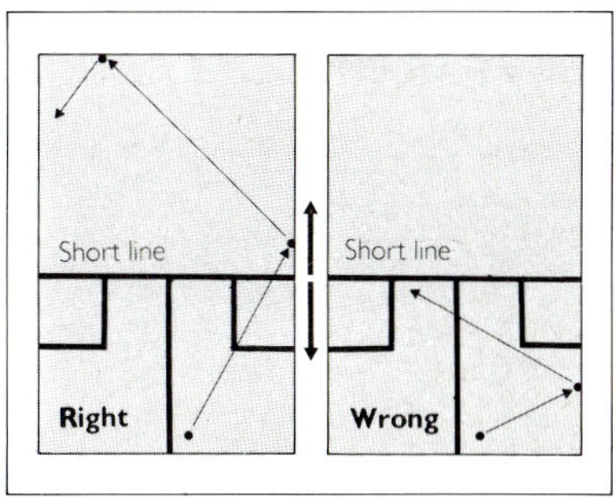

This shot is a means of defence that should be used only in certain circumstances. Try to develop a good 45° technique so that you are obliged to play the defensive boast only in an extreme emergency.

Special techniques

Once you have mastered the basic strokes it is time to learn some special techniques which you can then use to put your opponents under pressure. In this section we cover the following shots:

- Drop shot
- Trickle boast
- Lob
- Reverse boast
- Deflated volley boast
- Volleys: stop volley, nick volley, smash volley, reverse boast volley.

Attacking shots from the back: floating boast, hard boast, nick boast, back court drop shot, back court cross-court drop shot, back court reverse boast.

These special techniques make very great demands on players' skill and fitness. They go to make up a large part of advanced and expert players' training programmes and in competitive squash they are indispensable to successful match play.

But the more casual player, too, ought to practise these techniques systematically as their use makes playing squash much more fun.

Drop shot

Hard boast

Lob

Drop shot

Stop volley

Trickle boast

1

2

3

Drop shot

The drop shot is one of the most important attacking shots. The ball is played gently and just above the tin to make it land well to the front of the court. The shot should take your opponent by surprise.

On a drop shot the ball is not so much struck as pushed using a short swinging action.

Forehand drop shot

Backswing

- There is a minimal backswing.
- Take your racket arm, which should be bent, slightly back.
- Keep the racket head above your wrist.
- Tip your hand back at the wrist.

Impact

- Assume the same position as for the drive.
- Bend deeply at the knees.
- Hit the ball just in front of your body with a slight swinging action.
- Keep your wrist and arm tensed during the stroke.
- Give the ball a little bottom slice with the open racket face.

Follow-through

- Allow the racket to swing through in the direction of thc shot.
- Never play a rotating follow-through.

4

5

6

Important Ensure that the ball flies in an arc. If the ball flies flat and is played just above the tin

- the risk of an error is too great
- the ball will bounce too far back in the court.

If your opponent is at the back of the court you should always play a drop shot.

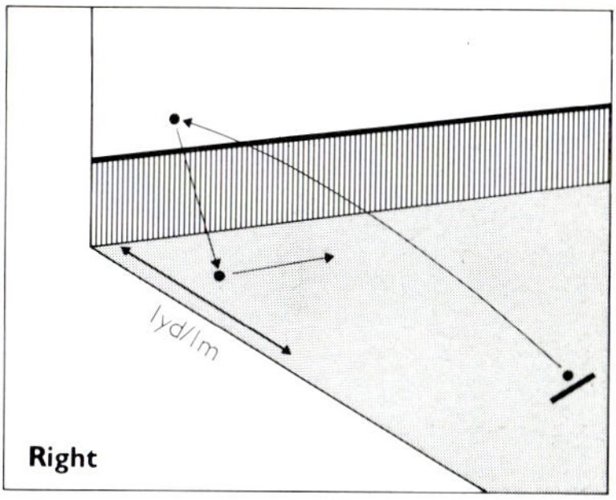

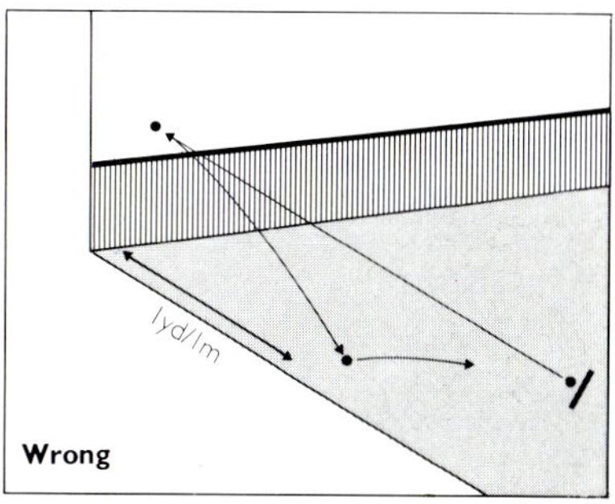

Drop shots as deception shots

In time you should try to develop a perfect deceptive drop shot tactic. To do so you mislead your opponent by setting up for a normal drive only to end up playing a drop shot.

Backhand drop shot

This is the same technique as for the forehand.

Important Remember to push the ball rather than strike it. Open the racket face by turning your forearm inwards.

Crosscourt drop shot

The ball is played diagonally across court, rather than straight, or down the length of it. The stroke technique is the same but the ball is simply played a little earlier than on a straight drop shot and your body should face the front wall more.

1

2

3

4

Important On a crosscourt drop shot you should make sure that the ball doesn't come off the front wall straight onto the side wall as this will send it right back into the centre of the court.

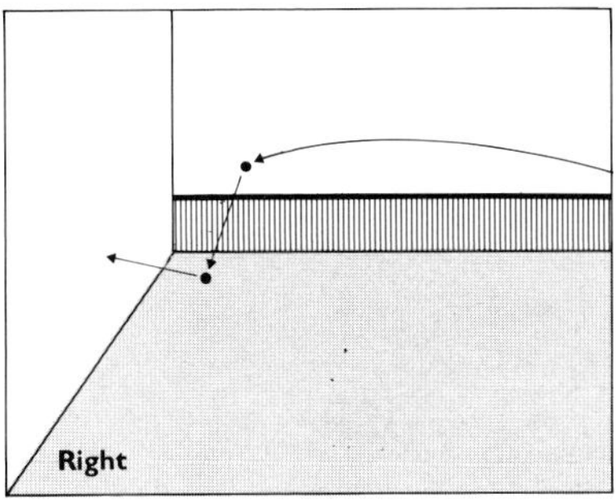

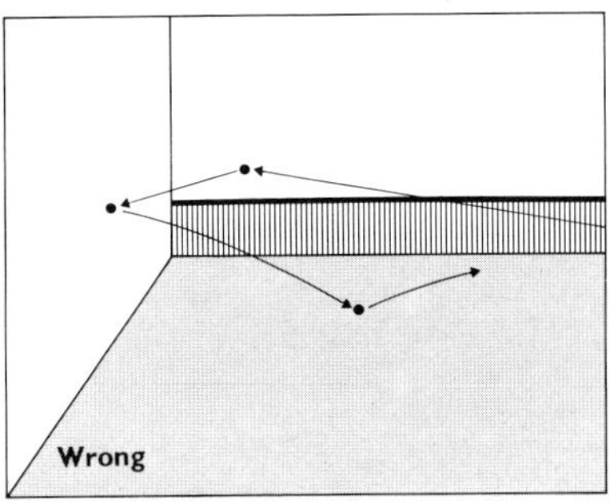

Experience shows that it is harder to return a straight drop shot than a crosscourt drop shot as the ball stays close to the side wall. Make most of your drop shots straight, keeping the crosscourt drop as an occasional effective surprise variation.

Left and right: Crosscourt drop shots

Trickle boast

The ball is played flat to just above the tin to make it bounce for the second time as quickly as possible. This shot looks like a drive right up to the point of impact. The trickle boast is strictly a deception shot and so very effective.

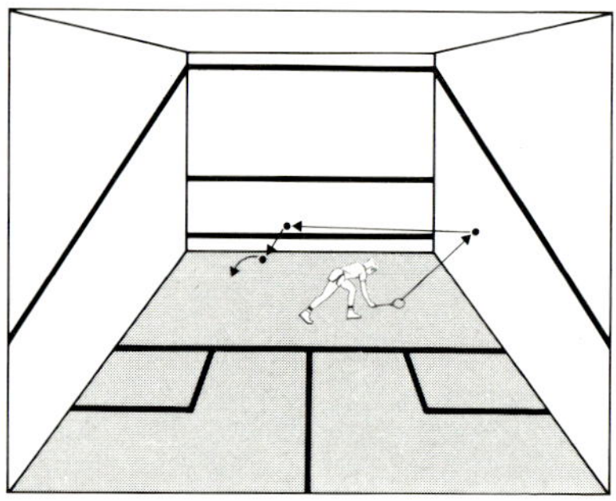

Ball's path on trickle boast

Backswing

- This is as for the drive.

Impact

- Assume a normal position.
- Bend deeply at the knees.
- Bend your hand back at the wrist so the racket face is very open.
- Turn your forearm inwards on the backhand.
- Cut the ball heavily with a short swing.
- Add some side spin to the ball by pulling your wrist through at a slight angle.

Follow-through

- The follow-through is short.

Important

- The stroke action should be fast.
- Don't strike the ball too firmly.
- The shot will be most effective if the ball travels to just above the tin.
- To prevent balls going out you must cut them heavily.

> Don't play the trickle boast very often. The shot is very effective when it comes as a surprise, but if your opponent is able to anticipate it its effectiveness is greatly diminished.

The difference in techniques between the drive and trickle boast is that the racket face is more open on the trickle boast than on the drive.

Left and right: Trickle boasts

Lob

In this technique the ball is played high and slow to the back of the court. A well placed lob is difficult to return, but unfortunately, the lob is one of the least played shots in squash.

The lob technique is very different from that for the drive. The lob is played mainly from the wrist.

Forehand lob

Backswing

- Use minimum backswing!
- Hold the racket in front of your body.
- Turn your forearm outwards.
- Tip your hand back at the wrist.

Impact

- With your body arched play the ball from well in front of you.
- Keep a good distance from the ball.
- Swing the racket under the ball using forearm and wrist action to keep the racket face wide open.
- Play the ball as high as possible onto the front wall.

Follow-through

- Follow-through upwards and forwards for a short distance.

Forehand (left) and backhand (right) lob sequences.

Backhand lob

This is as for the forehand except
- Bring your right shoulder forwards.
- Turn your forearm slightly inwards.
- Reach your racket arm out into the shot at impact.
- Use your forearm and wrist to lift the ball.

Important The lob must be played high and gently.

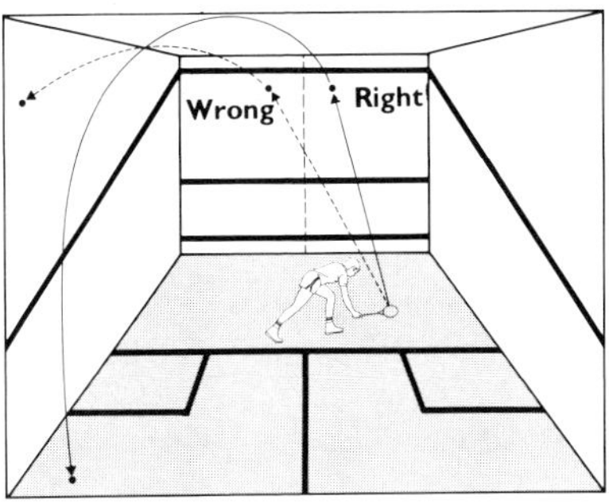

Backhand lob trajectories

Correcting faults

- Trajectory too flat, leaving your opponent with easy volley.
  Open your racket face wider and aim higher on the front wall.
- Ball going out or bouncing off back wall because stroke action too expansive.
  Play a more compact and gentler shot.
- Ball often going over side line and out.
  Play the ball more towards the centre of the front wall.

Reverse boast

As the name suggests, the ball isn't played onto the nearest wall but onto the opposite one. The reverse boast should be played as a surprise shot. The backswing should be such that a drive might be expected and then, during the impact phase, your wrist should be firmly flexed to the left in the forehand or to the right in the backhand.

Technique

Backswing

- This is the same backswing as for the drive.

Impact

- Take up the basic position.
- Lunge to the left.
- Strike the ball right in front of your body, not to the side, as for a lob.

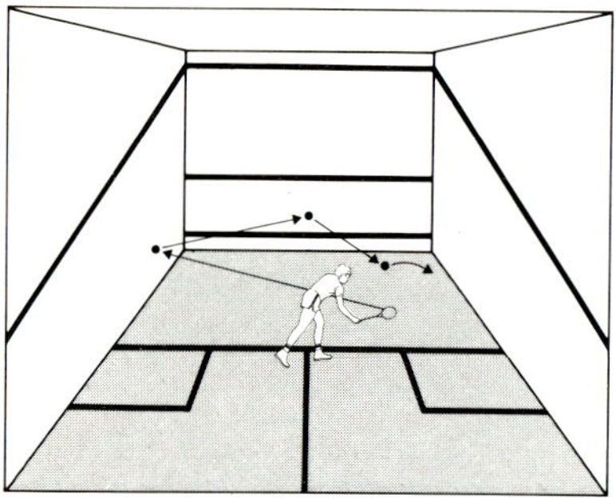

Above: Ball's path on reverse boast

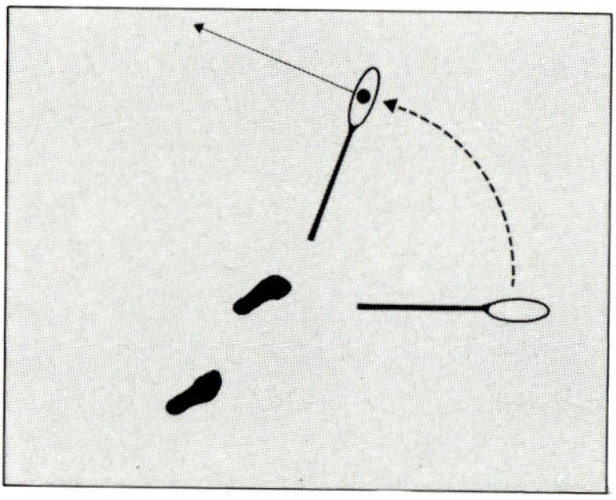

Above and below: Reverse boast technique

- Follow the normal stroke action until just before impact.
- Then pull your wrist sharply to the left (forehand) or right (backhand).
- Your racket face should be open to cut the ball slightly.

You should use this shot only rarely. If the reverse boast is played too often you can land yourself in tactical difficulties as your opponent can easily reach the ball.

Follow-through

- Swing the racket in a circle to your left (forehand) or right (backhand) shoulder.

Important The ball must be struck right in front of your body, otherwise it will be impossible to pull your wrist quickly to the side.

Don't forget to take up the same position as for the drive and to play the shot mainly from your wrist. Your opponent will easily see through it if you assume a head-on position.

Above: Reverse boast under pressure

4

5

6

Faded volley boast

The stroke technique is similar to the one for the straight volley. The stroke action is particularly short and compact.

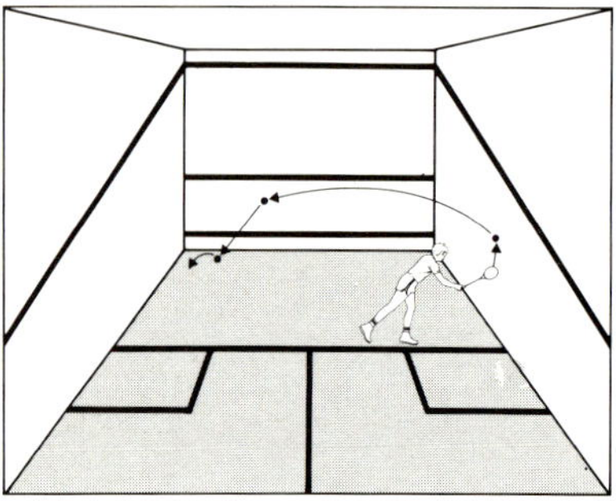

Ball's flight path on faded volley boast

Important The ball must be lifted onto the side wall using an open racket face. If the ball is hit correctly it isn't necessary to hit it hard.

As the ball is meant to land at the front of the court (as on the drop shot) it shouldn't be struck firmly. The trajectory from the side wall to the front wall must be curved and drop steeply in the final phase.

If the ball isn't lifted but played hard and flat against the side wall there is high risk of it landing in the tin. If the ball is hit high and hard against the side wall it will bounce back too far into the centre of the court.

1

1

Forehand and backhand examples

2

3

2

3

Stop volley

Technique

The technique is the same as for the drop shot.

Ideally, the stop volley should be played from shoulder height.

Important Although the ball is struck downwards in the air the racket face is kept open, which gives the ball back spin.

The risk of error on a stop volley is relatively high because the player has little time to execute the shot and it has to be aimed only just above the tin.
You should play a stop volley only if you can prepare it well enough. Otherwise, play a volley to the back of the court or a volley boast.

1

2

3

4

zenger

1

2

Nick volley and nick

A shot played into the angle between the side wall and the floor is called a nick. The ball doesn't bounce, but rolls along the floor. The nick is the most aggressive stroke in squash and obviously a well placed one cannot be returned.

Nick volley

- Unlike other volleys, which require a shortened stroke action, the nick volley action is like throwing a stone.
- For this stroke it is essential that your racket face is closed when it makes impact with the ball.
- Ideally, there should be no spin on the ball.
- During the stroke action shift your weight forwards.

Ball's flight path on nick volley.

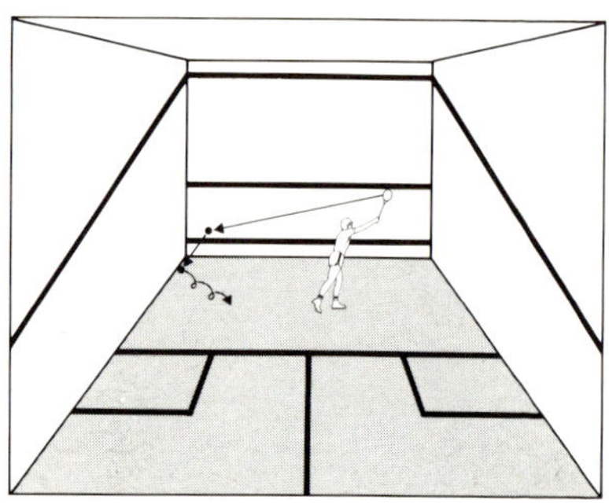

3

4

- Your racket-arm action is from the back and up to the front and down.
- The racket follows through to the front and down.

Nick

A nick can be also played after the ball has bounced from the floor.

- Use a normal drive action.
- Shift your weight far forwards.
- Strike the ball downwards with the racket face slightly closed.
- Hit it at its highest point.

Play a nick only from a secure position as it is one of the riskiest squash shots.

Rear-court attacking shots

Once you have mastered the 45° technique you will also be able to play attacking shots from the back of the court.

Floating boast

This boast isn't hit firmly but lifted lightly on to the side wall. The ball should bounce at the front of the court, as in a drop shot.

Ball's flight path on a floating boast.

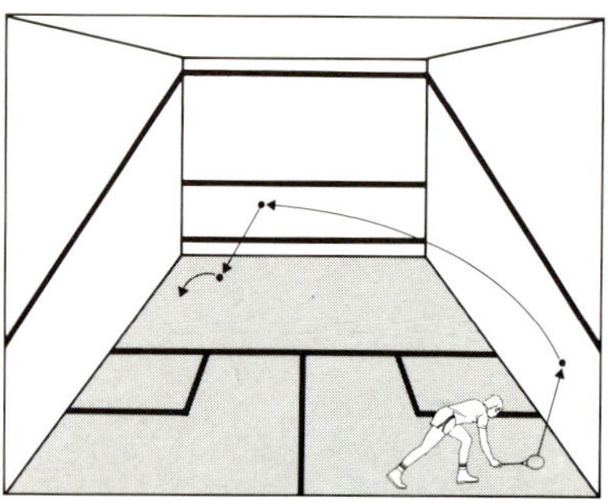

Technique

- The stroke technique is the same as for the 45° longline.
- The flight angle on to the side wall must be kept small so that the ball hits only two walls, the side and the front.

The aim of the floating boast is to force your opponent to run and to prepare for you to win the point on the next shot to the back of the court.

Advantages

- little energy required
- can be played with little time or space to spare
- minimal risk.

Hard boast

Technique

Use the floating boast technique but strike the ball firmly and aim for just above the tin.

Advantages

- possible winner
- surprise element

Disadvantages

- great deal of energy required
- requires space and time
- relatively risky

Nick boast (three-wall boast)

Technique

- Use the normal drive technique.
- The flight angle on to the side wall should be smaller than on other boasts.
- The ball must be played flat and hard.

Advantages

- possible winner
- difficult for opponent to return

Disadvantages

- as for hard boast

Play the hard boast or nick boast if your opponent
- is tired
- isn't standing right on the T
- isn't concentrating.

Ball's flight path on a nick boast.

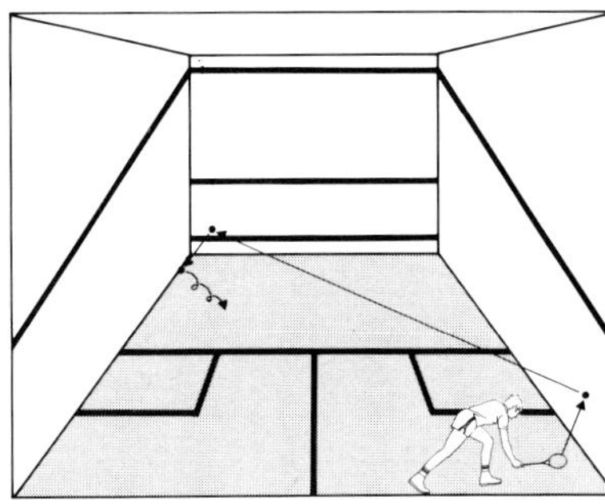

Special strokes from the rear

If a straight drive is struck too firmly the ball will travel to the back wall and bounce back into the centre of the court.

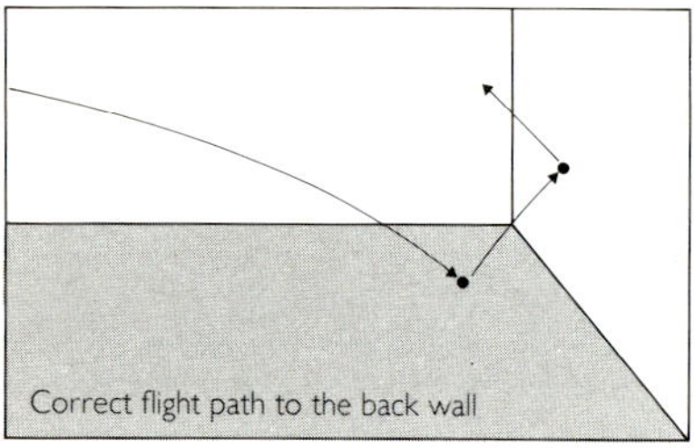

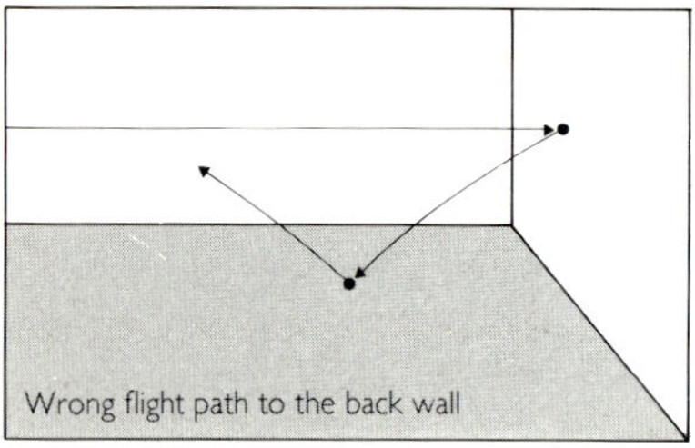

If your opponent has played such an unfortunate shot you will have no back corner problems. As a rule you will have plenty of time and space to attack your opponent with a firm longline or crosscourt drive.

However, interesting variations to straight or crosscourt drives are:

- Drop shot from the back of the court
- Crosscourt drop shot from the back of the court
- Reverse boast from the back of the court

Back-court drop shot

An important factor in the success of this shot is disguising it as a straight drive.

Technique

- The deception is achieved by exaggerating the backswing.
- The apparent delivery is altered during the stroke action; in the impact phase use the drop shot procedure.
- Cut the ball by keeping your wrist tensed.

Important
The difference between the drop shot and the back court drop shot is that in the drop shot there is a curved trajectory and slight cut whereas on the back court drop shot there is a straight trajectory and heavy cut.

Back-court crosscourt drop shot

This drop shot is a deceptive shot which, if properly executed, will leave your opponent without any chance of returning. Your opponent must mistakenly believe that you will play a straight drop shot. To strengthen this belief you must have played some straight drops previously.

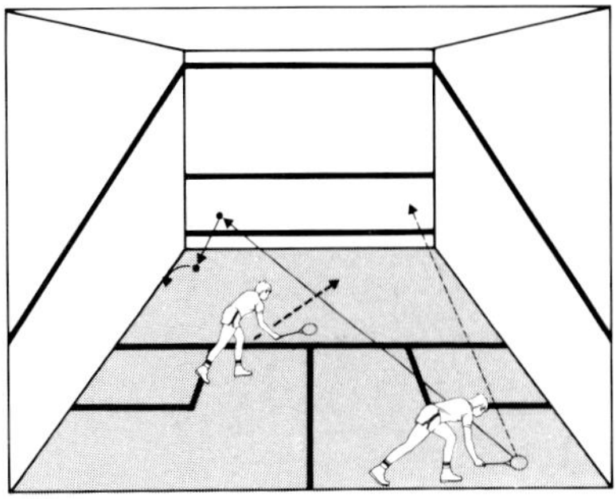

Crosscourt drop shot

Technique

- The backswing on the crosscourt drop shot is, unlike that on the back court drop shot, as for a normal drop shot with a reduced backswing.
- Assume the normal sideways-on position.
- Your backswing movement and body position should indicate a straight drop shot.
- Hold back the stroke action for as long as possible so that your opponent starts to run to the front right corner.
- Hit the ball well in front of your body.
- Play the ball into the bottom left corner by using an open racket face and gentle swing.

Important
As the back court crosscourt drop shot is, without doubt, a surprise shot, the tactical rule applies to it too: use it sparingly!

Back-court reverse boast

As with the back court drop shot, your opponent should believe you intend to play a straight drive.

Technique

- Make a normal backswing.
- Take up a sideways-on position.
- Hit the ball in front of your body.
- Use a strong wrist action.
- Play the ball strongly to the right.

Serving

In squash there are a number of different types of serve.

Standard serves
- Flat serve
- Lob serve

Special serves
- Serve to the centre
- Bodyline serve
- Corkscrew serve

Essentially, beginners and advanced players should opt for the flat serve, which is the safest to play.

Take your time when serving. It is the only time you will be able to prepare your shot unhurried.

Standard serves

Flat serve (forehand)

The aim of all flat serves is to force your opponent to play a defensive return.

Technique

- The technique is as for the volley.
- The ball is played to hit the wall about 3 feet/1 metre above the cut

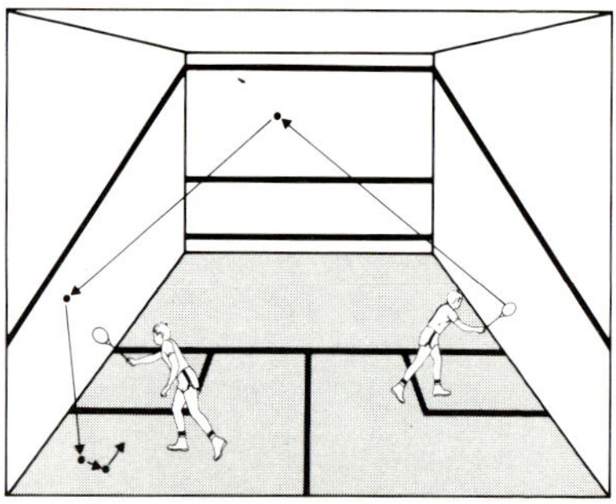

Ball's path on a flat serve

or service line (see illustration).

- The ball should hit the side wall (behind the service box) to prevent your opponent playing an easy return volley.

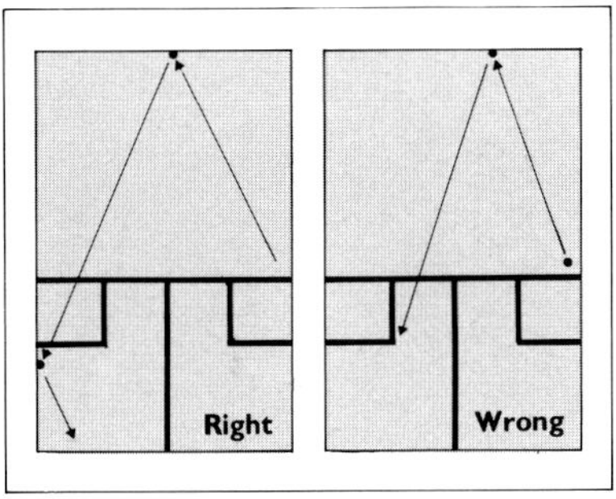

Forehand flat-serve angles

Correcting faults

- Ball flying straight into opponent's quarter of court without hitting side wall.
  Alter flight angle (see illustration).
- Ball going out.
  Strike the ball with less force and don't open the racket face too wide.
- Ball bouncing too far from back wall.
  Strike the ball with less force.
- Flight too short.
  Strike the ball with more force and open the racket face wider.
- Ball hitting front wall below cut or service line.
  Open the racket face more.

Tips for beginners

If you are failing to make satisfactory contact with the ball when serving it is because you haven't got the distance right between your hand holding the ball and the hand holding the racket.

1

2

Flat serve (backhand)

The flat serve can also be played on the backhand.

That said, you should only serve on the backhand when serving from the right service box.

Advantages

- The flight angle is smaller – the ball stays closer to the side wall.
- You can watch your opponent while serving.
- When serving you are only one step away from the T.

Beginners should first master playing the forehand flat serve.

Technique

- The stroke technique is as for the backhand volley.
- The ball is played further to the left on the front wall than on the forehand serve.
- While serving your right leg should be well in front of your left, and both feet should be almost parallel to the short line.

Ideal flight path on a backhand flat serve

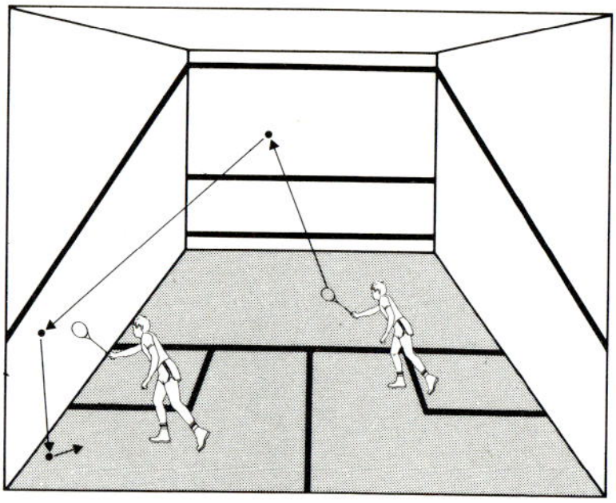

3

4

Perfect execution of the backhand flat serve

Lob serve

The lob serve is a risky shot so you should only play it when you feel confident and can afford a potential loss of serve. Otherwise stick to the flat serve. The lob serve is only played on the forehand.

Important Avoid the lob serve if the ball is very warm. Its high bounce off the back wall makes it easy for your opponent to return, and there is also the danger of hitting it out.

Technique

- The lob serve technique is the same as for the lob.
- Throw the ball up directly in front of your body and play it at about hip height.
- Stand right at the front of the service box so as to get the steepest angle possible to the front wall.
- Serve with your left leg forward.
- The ball should drop as nearly vertically as possible from your opponent's back wall.

Serving from the left

Lob serve from the right

1 2

3

4

Match tactics

You should try to assess both your own and your opponent's abilities well in advance of a match. Watching and analysing match play will help you do this.

Basic tactical principles

Play safe

Experience shows that many matches are won on opponents' mistakes. Always play the ball safely over the tin and avoid unnecessary risks.

Fight for every ball

No matter how far behind you are you should always fight for every ball. The match isn't over until after the last point.

Don't change tactics for no reason

Don't change the way you are playing unless your tactics have proved to be unsuccessful.

Maintain a good position on the ball

Accurate and safe shots can only be played if you have a good position on the ball. This means you should concentrate on developing good foot work, running technique and physical fitness.

Concentrate on your serve

When serving you must remember that you have the advantage. So take your time, concentrate and don't play rashly.

Force your opponent to run

This will succeed best if you play to all four corners of the court, using random sequences of well varied shots. Your opponent will tire quickly and play more uncontrolled shots under pressure.

Never play across your opponent's reach

You opponent will be able to play controlled shots from a stationary position, and you will have no time to gain the T.

Keep your eye on the ball

Disguised shots and deceptions are less dangerous if you see the ball early.

Recognise and exploit your opponents' weaknesses

For instance

- Make unfit players run a lot.
- Play to the backhand of players with weak backhands.
- Attack players with poor back corner techniques by playing long shots.

Recognise your opponents' strengths

- Don't give your opponents the opportunity to play their best shots.
- Notice the shots your opponents play frequently.

Make surprise attacks

Play the occasional unexpected attacking shot when a safety shot would be expected. However, don't do so too often otherwise the surprise element will be lost. Also, the attack shouldn't be too hurried or it will be doomed to failure from the start.

Vary the tempo of the game

Keep changing the ball speed to prevent your opponent finding rhythm.

As well as fitness and technical skill, your attitude in play is a very important factor.

- Always concentrate on the match.
- Never underestimate your opponent.
- Play without excessive stress.
- Never get annoyed – only your opponent will be pleased.
- Put your mistakes behind you.
- Play optimistically.
- Always play to win, never give up.
- Play fairly.
- Praise your opponent when he wins a good point.

Important: keep your eye on the ball

Important: play dynamically

Building an attack

Experience shows that the greatest success is achieved if your scoring is planned and prepared.
The following tactical principles must be followed rigidly:

- Win control of the T.
- Put your opponent under pressure with good length shots to the back of the court.
- Wait for a bad shot from your opponent (shots that land too short or bounce in the centre of the court).
- Play an attacking shot in response to a bad shot.
- If your opponent can block your attack try to regain control of the T.

Important For a successful winning shot you will need

- a shot ripe for attack
- for your opponent to be in a weak position.

Don't try to win the point too early

- if you attack off unsuitable shots (e.g. good length, close to the wall) you will make too many errors,
- opponents in too good a position have too much time to reach the ball and begin an attack themselves.

Readiness and action during match play

Length

By length we refer to distances between the front and back walls. A good length ball is one that bounces in the furthest recesses of the court near the back wall.

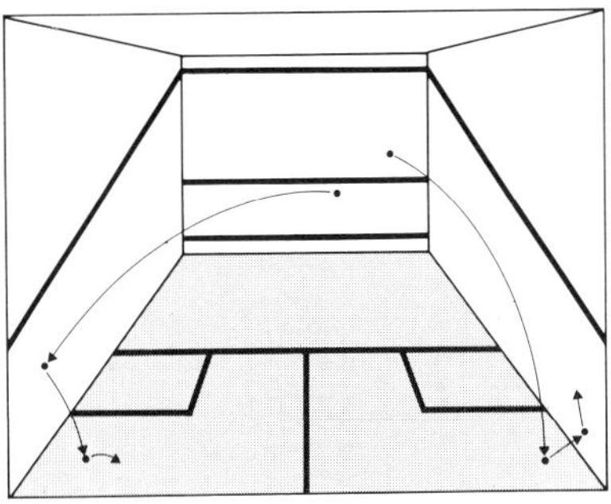

Good length is essential for building pressure into your game. It forces your opponent to the back of the court, and so to surrender the T and thus

- you will control the T
- your opponent's attack will be severely diminished
- you can build your own attack.

Without good length your opponents will rarely be put under pressure, which will leave them free to build their own attack.

Important To develop good length you will need a technically sound drive.

To improve length try playing high onto the front wall.

Width

By width we mean always playing the ball close to the side wall so as to leave your opponent with as little room as possible for a shot.

Important As a rule, you should never play the ball to the centre of the court. Such shots will give your opponent a decisive advantage.

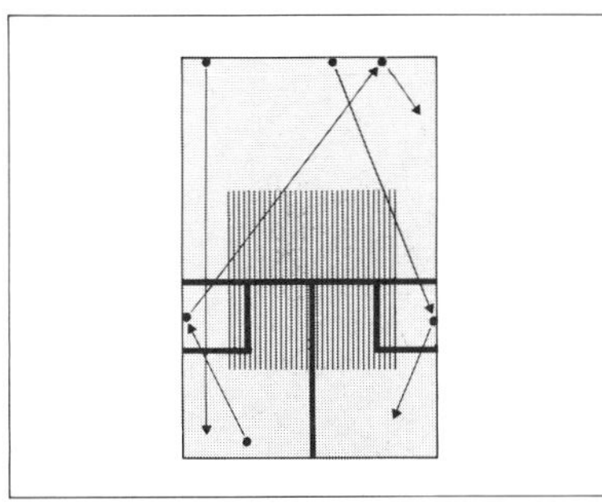

Start of play

There is an increasing tendency in modern squash for the tactics and techniques of the serve and return of serve to have a great influence on the outcome of matches.

As a rule the server has the greater opportunity for determining the course of the following rally.

Serving

- Play the service unhurriedly and with concentration.
- Leave your opponent unsure of what type of serve you will play.
- Use a successful serve again.
- Use surprise serves sparingly (serve to the centre, bodyline serve).
- Only play serves you have thoroughly mastered.
- Observe your opponent's position before you serve.
- Take no risks on a second serve.

Serving position

The positions are described in detail in the descriptions of the individual serving techniques.

Concentrating on the serve

Return of serve

The return of serve plays a very important part in match tactics. This return determines:

- who will reach the T first
- who will have the first chance to attack

The standard reply to a serve is a long, safe straight volley to the back of the court.

This will

- force the server to the back
- give control of the T
- avoid possible difficulties in the back corner.

Preparing to receive

Position for returning serve

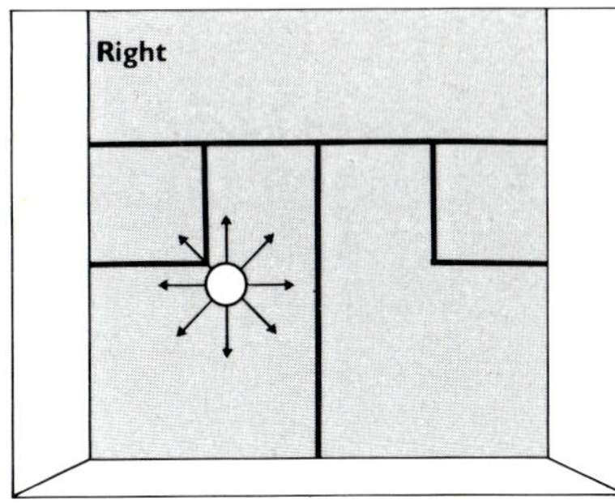

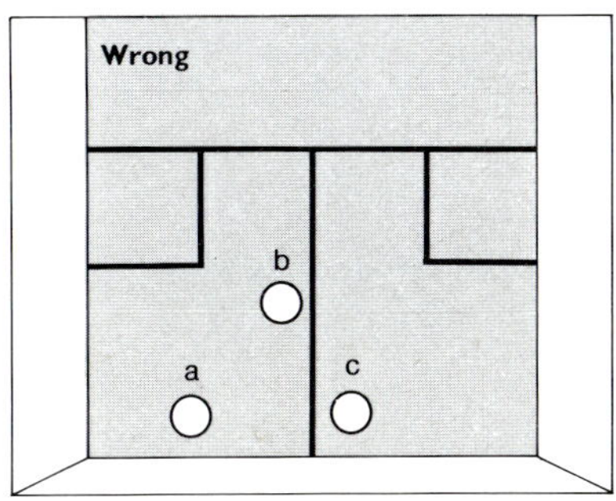

Volley return

- Use a normal volley technique.
- Lift the ball high onto the front wall with an open racket face.
- Make the shot short and gentle.

Don't hit the ball hard; experience shows that the number of balls that either go into the tin or are easily returned by an opponent is very high.

Definition

By training we mean all the elements that go towards improving your technical, tactical, physical and mental abilities.

Training should provide you with

- Enjoyable activity
- Fun and companionship
- Fitness and well being
- Personal targets to achieve

Ten golden rules for training

1 Train regularly.

2 Train systematically and to a plan.

3 Be concentrated and determined in your training.

4 Enjoy your training and expect to see progress.

5 Don't overdo your training.

6 Keep calm.

7 Help organise your training.

8 Analyse and correct your mistakes.

9 Don't train if you are ill or injured.

10 Keep a record of your training and matches (enter the results of your training and matches, make a note of training sessions).

Based on current understanding and knowledge of training, we can say

- Training can help cultivate and develop both physical and mental abilities.
- You should start to train early on and should train using different varied activities.
- Training should be devised and organised according to a long-term plan.
- The amount of training you do will be determined by your age, your general fitness, your willingness to train and your opportunities to do so regularly.

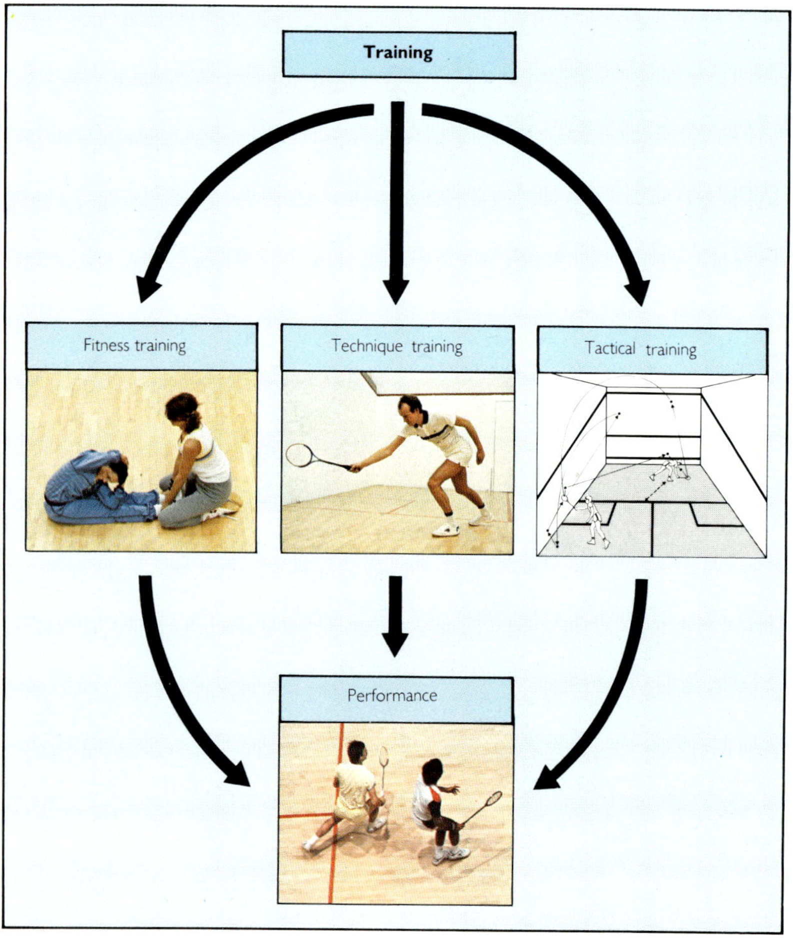

To get a realistic picture of your general physical fitness you can do training tests or play matches. You can achieve a good fitness level with a combination of different activities: training exercises on particular points, playing in different types of competitive matches and by general fitness training, using different exercises and equipment.
Remember that as long as training is fun you must be doing it along the right lines.

Organising your training

If you are to enjoy your training and see measurable results for your efforts you need to organise all aspects of it in a planned and sensible way.

Essentially there are two key elements in organising training:

- The content and structure of training sessions
- Training phases

Before training can begin you will also need to take account of all that goes into training.
This includes:

- The number of hours a week you can devote to training
- Who is available to help you
- Facilities
- The number and type of people taking part
- Your standard of performance.

Training session breakdown

Every training session should consist of three parts:

- Warm-up
- Main section
- Final part

Warm-up

This is to tune up your body.

Exercises

Always begin with some gentle running, followed by running and jumping exercises, gymnastics, work on your reactions and, finally, some sprinting.

This should take up 10% of total time.

Main section

For improving your technical and tactical squash abilities.

Exercises

Squash techniques and tactics. 60% of total time should be devoted to the main section.

Final part

Finally you should concentrate on turning technical and tactical, physical and mental abilities into sound match play performance.

Exercises

All forms of match play. This should take up 30% of the session.

Training phases

At club and national levels of the sport it is essential to divide the year's training programme into separate periods. It has proved useful to divide the squash year into three phases.

- preparation period
- competition period
- transitional period

The preparation period should be mainly concerned with improving your general fitness. During the competition period tactical and technical work should be given priority and during the transitional period there should be a relaxed winding down involving playing other sports.

If you don't keep to these training periods there is a danger of over-training, characterised by listlessness, lack of commitment and general loss of interest.

Important
It is obvious that, if you are not playing highly competitive squash, you don't need such a strict training programme as the more advanced players; but you should follow the general outlines; if you play nothing but squash you are likely to get the same symptoms as over-training. For competitive players training must be planned in such a way that their peak performance coincides with major events. The graph below shows the performance peaks and troughs for the average competitive player throughtout a typical year.

Training effort

An important factor when drawing, up a training plan is co-ordinating

Performance capacity during each period.

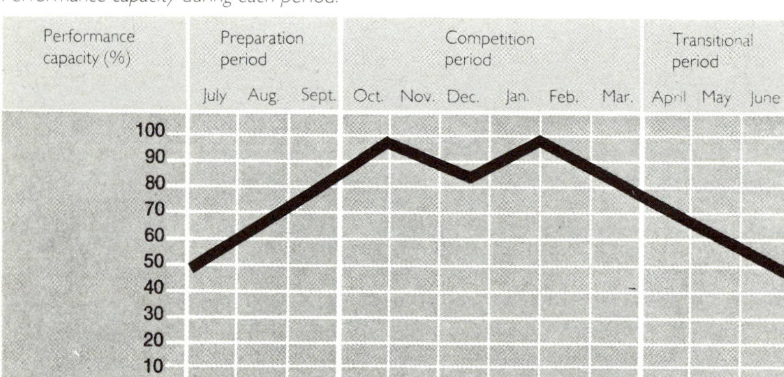

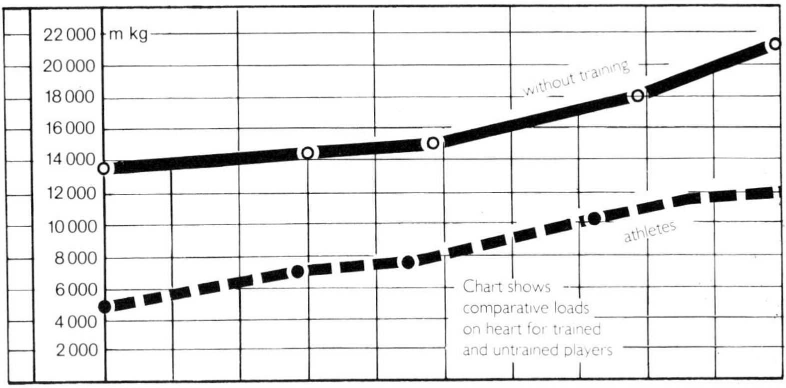

your training methods with your training effort. How hard you train will depend on

- Your age and gender
- The standard you have reached and your physical fitness
- The level and intensity at which you play
- The temperature and time of day

Excessive exertion will cause a

- Slowly falling pulse rate
- Markedly pallid complexion

and later reactions of

- Tiredness
- Weakness
- Listlessness

If you notice such reactions you should train less vigorously or for a shorter time in future.

Pulse measurement

You can take your pulse on the inside of your wrist using your index and middle finger, at the carotid artery in your neck, or with the flat of your hand placed directly over your heart. Count the number of beats over a 15-second period and multiply this number by four to get the pulse rate per minute. While training you should first measure your pulse rate immediately after exertion and take a second measurement 3 minutes later.

The greater the difference between the first and second readings the better your physical condition. A healthy athlete should have measurements of about 150 beats a minute on the first reading, and 120 beats a minute on the second reading and, after 5 minutes, about 90 beats a minute.

Important
For training to have any long-term effect, a fit sports player will need to achieve pulse rates of 140-160 beats a minute while exercising. During very intensive training or competition the pulse rate can rise to as much as 180-200 beats a minute. Such loads can only be sustained for short periods (2-5 minutes).

Beginner's training

When people begin playing squash they often find it more difficult than they thought it would be. The best way of getting started and getting used to the racket and ball is to try out some ball exercises.

Ball exercises

- Hold the racket with the correct grip and tap the ball into the air with the racket.
- Tap the ball, alternating between forehand and backhand.
- Tap the ball while walking and running.
- Use your racket to pick up the ball from the floor.
- Catch the ball on your racket.

Practise these ball exercises at home, too.

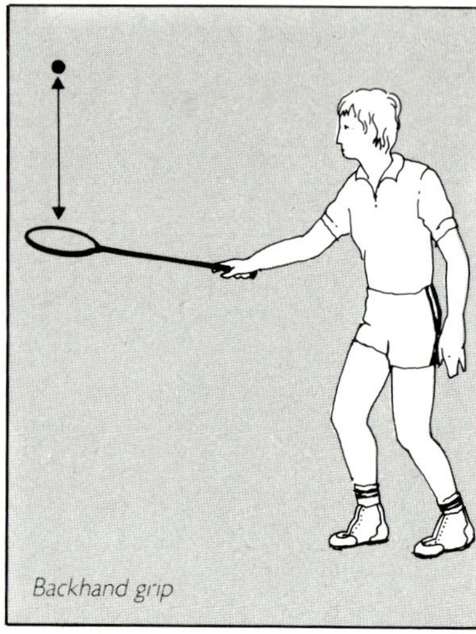

Tapping the ball

Important tips for beginners

Ball

Always play with blue dot balls. These bouncy balls are made specially for beginners and should always be used. Their advantages are that

- They don't need to be hit hard to warm them up.
- Their bounciness means that even beginners will, as a rule, be able to hit them.

Grip and holding the racket
Always check and correct.

Stance and position
By constantly moving, try to ensure that you are always side on to the ball when playing strokes.

Drive technique
Make sure that
- your backswing is fast and early
- your arm is angled on backswing
- the follow-through on the shot isn't rotating.

Mental training
Every beginner, and particularly when first starting practical squash training, should mentally run through their drive technique at home over and over again. This helps enormously.

Practising basic drives

The aim here is to practise basic positions, sound ball striking and correct technique.

Getting the ball into play
Get the ball into play by throwing it gently against the side wall with your free hand. Then play the ball onto the front wall off the bounce.

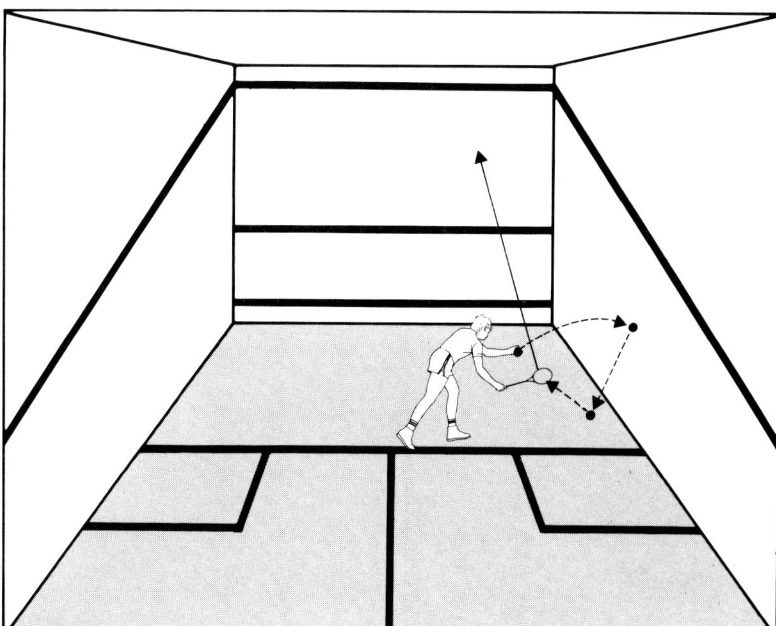

Important
- Don't strike the ball hard.
- The ball should hit the service line. Never try to play just over the tin.
- Don't play too close to the side wall: keep 3 feet (1metre) distance.

- If at all possible, practise with a trainer.
- Set specific targets for your shots (five shots without error, say).
- Don't get disheartened or annoyed if everything doesn't go right first time.

Types of training

Training sessions must never be monotonous and using varied types of training is the best guarantee that training will be both interesting and fun. Above all, it will guarantee fast and steady progress. Ideally varied types of training are possible when learning squash. It's particularly useful that you can practise
- alone
- in pairs
- in threes
- in fours

on one court. Also, you can choose from the following types of directions on the shot:
- parallel (straight)
- diagonal (crosscourt)
- half-court line
- front-wall zone
- back-wall zone.

These directions can then be varied as follows:
- short – long
- fast – slow
- gentle – hard
- deep – high
- forehand – backhand

When you consider the full range of service and other strokes that can be added to the above you will appreciate the many ways there are of making your training sessions interesting.

Important tips
- When training, the principles of system and planning must always be priorities. Always play every shot with the aim of making no mistakes.
- Each type of training exercise should last for an average of 10 minutes. If you realise that you are making a lot of mistakes before this time is up stop the exercise early.
- You will make progress fastest if you have a coach. However, your partner or another observing player can give you very useful advice.

Training aids

- films
- photos
- video recordings
- charts
- specialist literature
- ball feed machines

should be used in any planned training. In particular, charts detailing stroke techniques and a good squash book showing the many variations possible should always be to hand.

To make them easier to remember we have given most of the training exercises pithy names (e.g. 'triangle', 'egg-timer', etc.).

Ball-feed machine

Although ball-feed machines have been available as an essential training aid for table tennis and, particularly, for tennis players, for a long time, they are only slowly beginning to make headway in squash. The reason for this is that the machines have only recently been developed to an adequate level. There is no doubt that a ball-feed machine is an excellent aid but its usefulness shouldn't be overestimated.

Advantages

- Precise feeding
- Multiple feed variations
- High training intensity

Its greatest advantage, however, is in freeing coaches from the task. With a ball-feed machine the trainer can concentrate on essential tasks:

- teaching technique and tactics
- correcting errors

Ball-feed machines should be bought by sports centre owners or clubs or anywhere providing courses in squash.

Concentrated training

Solo training

Squash techniques lend themselves to solo training and you should certainly make the most of this possibility. You can practise particularly effectively alone on

- Stroke techniques
- Combination shots

Important Even if two people are practising together on a court you should devote the first 20 minutes of the session to solo training.

Advantages

- You become quickly accustomed to the equipment (ball, racket, court)
- Intensive learning results
- Excellent technique training.

Solo training exercises

Solo straight

Strokes: drive or volley, or alternating drive/volley

- Play safe
- Concentrate on technique
- Increase tempo
- Two players can play at the same time

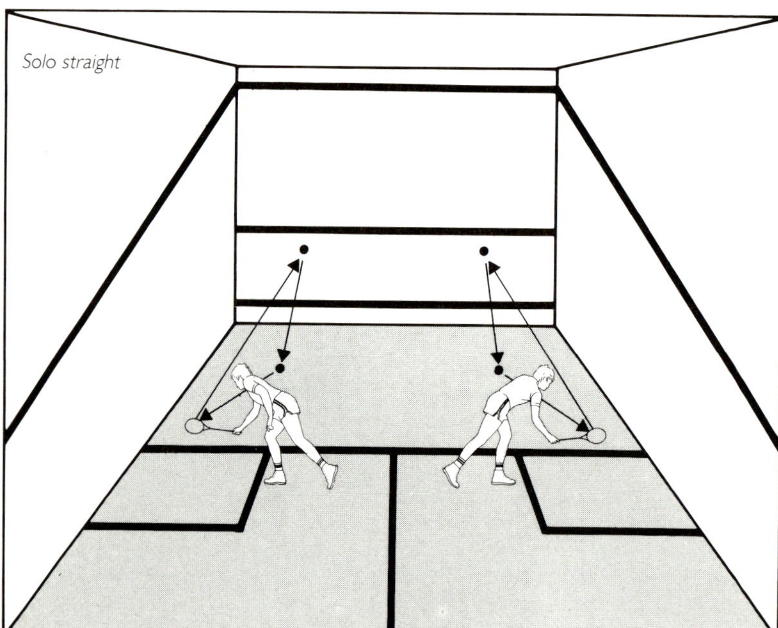

Double corner
Stroke: drive
Direction: see illustration
Side of racket: alternating from forehand to backhand

- Begin to drive slowly
- Use lots of footwork
- The point of impact on the ball should be on the front side above the service line.

Solo cross
Strokes: drive or volley, or alternating between forehand volley/backhand volley.

- Try to hit 50 shots with no errors
- Change position
  – play in front of the T
  – play near the front wall
  – play from the back

One corner
Stroke: driving boast
Direction: across to one corner
Side of racket: alternating from forehand to backhand

- Start off very slowly
- Hit increasingly tighter, lower and harder into the corner

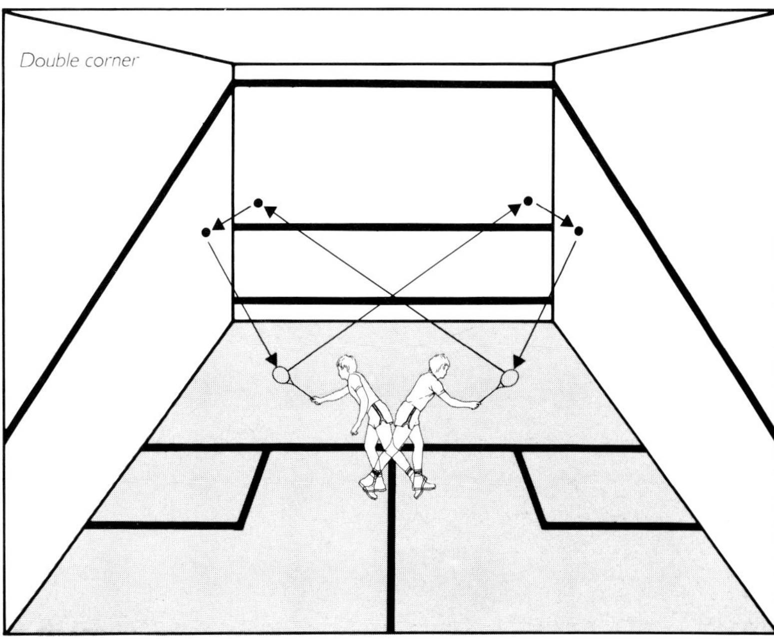

Double boast

Stroke: boast
Side of racket: forehand and backhand, alternating every 5 minutes.

Important: you can practise a hard drive here

- Start off slowly and play the ball high
- Increase tempo and place the ball lower

45° technique

Stroke: 45° technique
Direction: straight
Side of racket: forehand and backhand, alternating every 5 minutes.

- Always include this very important solo exercise in your training schedule
- Vary the height of the shot and flight
- Concentrate on a good length

Lengthwise shovel

Stroke: drive
Side of racket: alternating from forehand to backhand

- Vary strength of shot and height of flight

Note: 'shovel' from the way the player alternates 'shovelling' the ball on to the front or back wall.

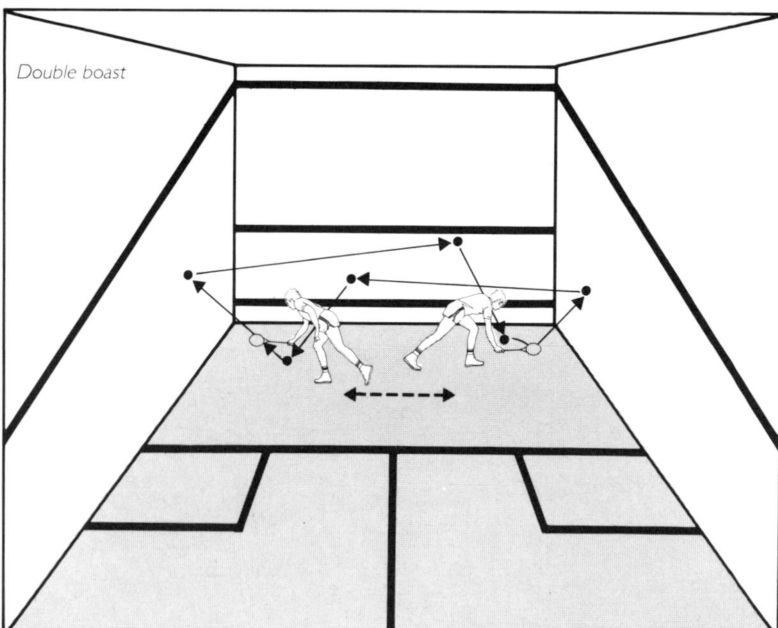

Egg-timer

Stroke: drive
Direction: alternating from straight to crosscourt
Side of racket: alternating from forehand to backhand every 5 minutes.

- Play with great concentration
- Aim for good placement
- Improve your foot work
- Take up the right position on the shot.

Serve and return

Strokes:
– Serves: flat serve to the front wall
– Returns: high gentle volley return
Direction: straight
Remember to take your time on the service; this is the only shot where you will be under no time pressure.

Important You should include specific service and return practice in every training session. Concentrate on your

- readiness position
- placement

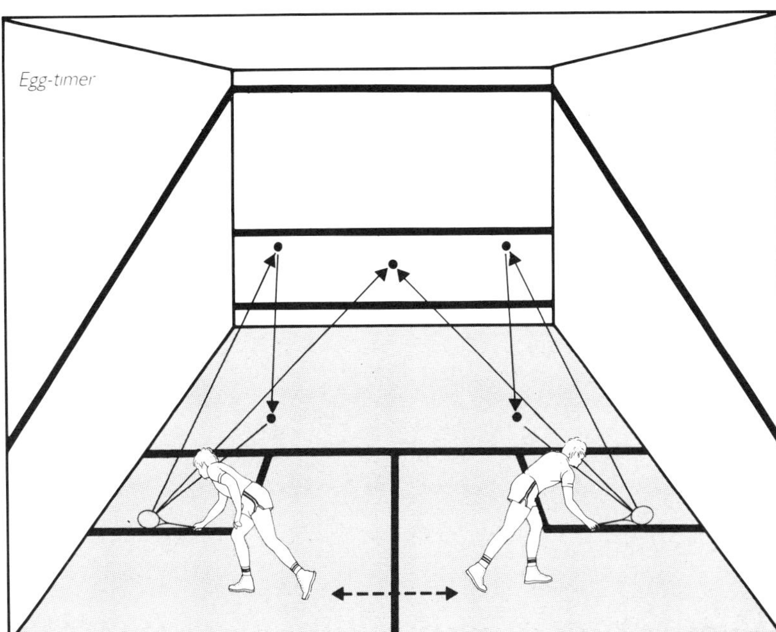

Complex exercise techniques

Straight and crosscourt

Also try to invent new complex exercise techniques.

Strokes

- Once again, drive and crosscourt drop shot from the back and drop shot and lob
- Then start from the other side

> - Sprint fast when running onto the crosscourt drop shot from the back.

Longline

Strokes

- Twice each, drive and volley and stop volley and drop shot
- Then lob to the back and start with a drive again

> - Start off playing slowly and cautiously
> - Don't play frantically when changing technique
> - Alter stroke techniques
> - Relax after finishing the rally

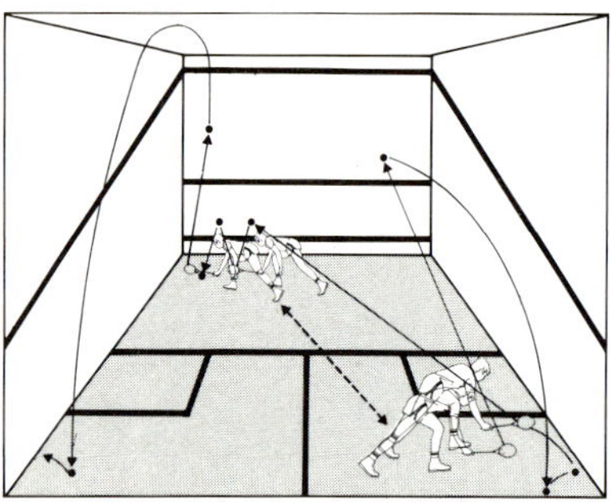

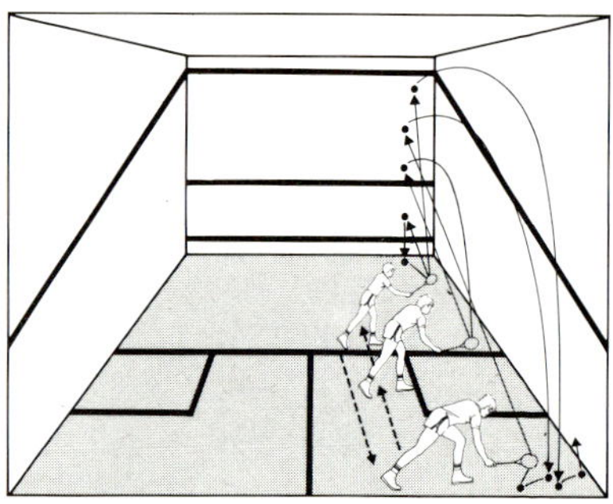

Pairs training

The most effective way of training is in pairs using the whole court. This is because

- There is lots of ball contact and so intensive training.
- You can get practice in all the technical and tactical demands of squash.
- There is interplay of shots across the whole court and you use a variety of running techniques.

There are three main areas of multiple-shot training, as follows:

Stroke techniques and combinations of shots

In this the type and direction of shots is determined in advance. The purpose is to improve specific weaknesses in stroke making.

Complex exercises

In contrast to the combination-shot exercises the sequence of strokes isn't determined in advance, though the types of strokes are. This increases the demands on the players, calling for increased concentration and commitment.

Rallies

Along with the complex exercises, rallying should also take up a major part of the main section of any training session. While rallying, players become familiar with standard matchplay situations and will remember them. It also provides an opportunity to assess and refine a variety of tactical ploys.

Carrying out exercises

- Each player should practise the exercise for 5 minutes.
- Individual strokes should be practised on the backhand as well as the forehand.
- Pay attention to your coach's comments on your performance and respond to them.
- To start with, the emphasis in all exercises should be on doing them accurately.
- Everyone should try to invent new exercises.

Boast – crosscourt combination

- A plays a boast from the back corner
- B plays a crosscourt from the front
- Starting position for A and B is the T position.

Run on to the ball in as few steps as possible.

Boast – drive combination

- A plays a boast from the back
- B plays a straight drive
- Always return to the T after the shot

Variations

- A plays a volley boast
- B feeds a straight drive

Volley stroke

- A plays a backhand volley
- B plays a forehand volley

Variations

- Instead of the volley play a drive
- A plays a stop volley from the back
- B plays a crosscourt drive from the front

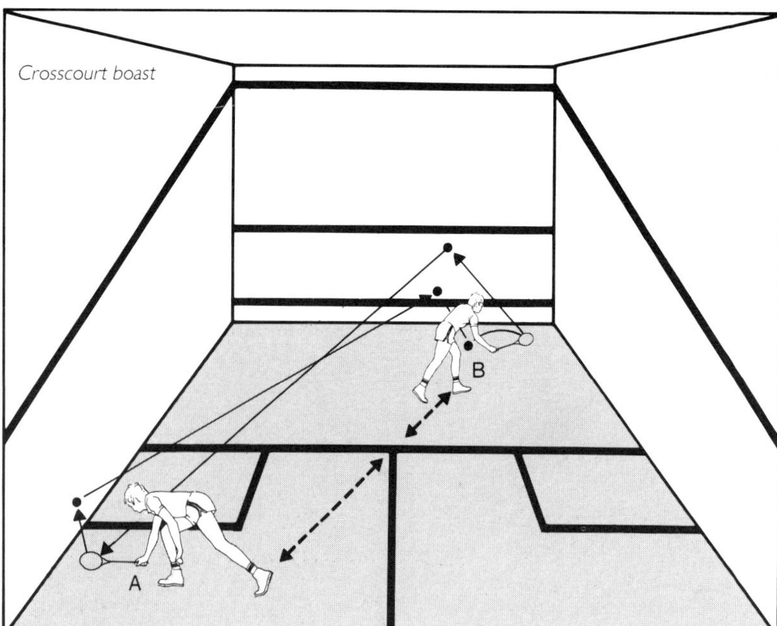

45° technique

- Both players play drives using the 45° technique
- Always return to the T after the shot

2 straight drives, 1 boast

- A plays a drive from the front
- B plays a drive from the back
- A plays a boast from the back
- B plays a drive from the front
- A plays a drive from the back
- B plays a boast from the back
- Begin the sequence again.

Drop shot from back, drive from front

- A feeds various length balls to B
- B returns them all as drop shots from the back

Use a racket, line, adhesive tape, or stick to mark the spot where you want the ball to land off the front wall, which should be about 3 feet/1 metre from it.

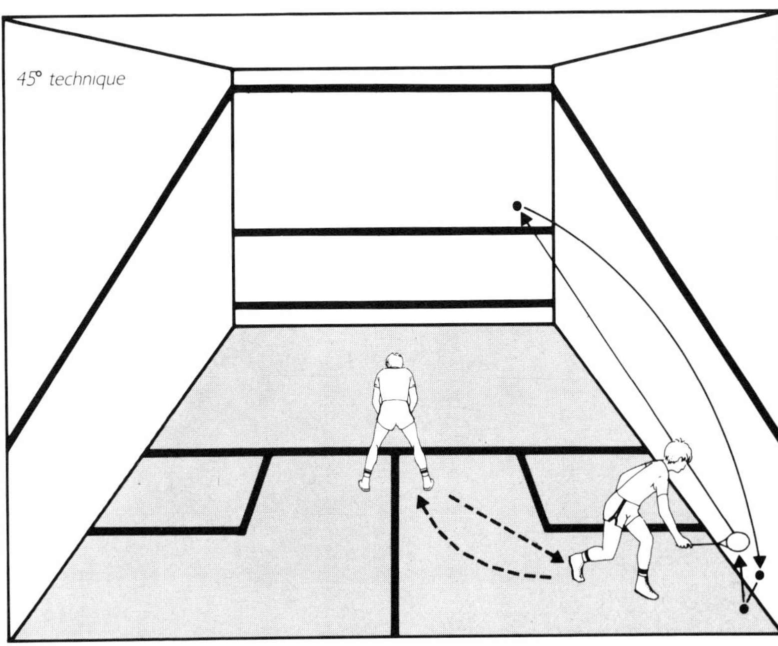

Lob – volley – boast
- A plays a lob
- B plays a straight volley
- B plays a boast to A

Begin the sequence again

Trickle boast – drop shot
- A plays a trickle boast
- B plays a drop shot
- Once you have played your shot run to the other side.

Variation: complex exercise
B plays several straight volleys or drives before feeding the boasts to A.

Complex exercises

Back wall
- Both players play long shots to make the ball bounce near the back wall.
- Stroke technique and direction are up to them.

Volleyed lob boast

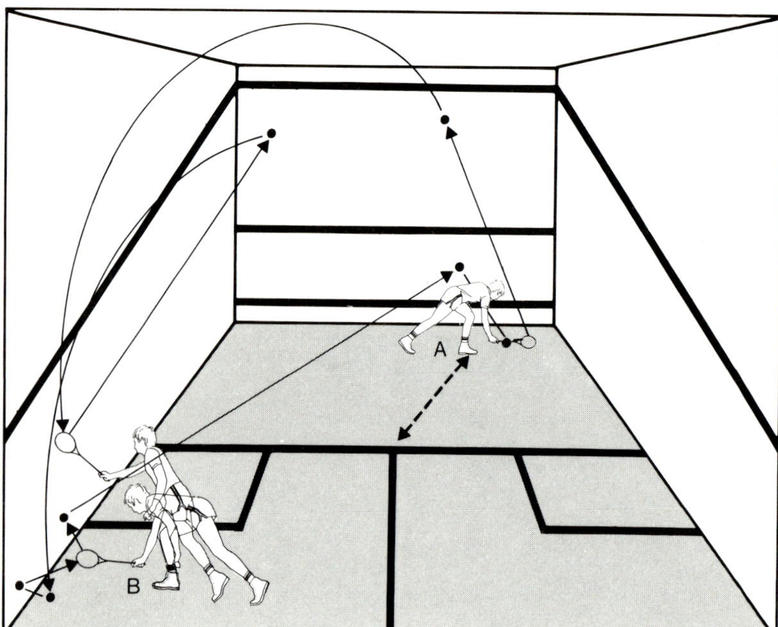

Side wall
- Both players are only allowed to play shots near the side wall.
- Stroke techniques are up to them.
- Always run to the T after the shot.

Placement
- A can play the ball anywhere
- B can only play it to the back

Gentle/hard
- A can only play gentle shots
- B can only play hard shots
- Do not forget to run to the T

Rally practice

As has already been mentioned in the introduction to pairs training, rally practice is essential. It should be used to practise standard match play situations and tactical behaviour. Practise the following pre-arranged series of strokes

1st rally
- A: lob serve from right
- B: volley (straight)
- A: drive (straight)
- B: stop volley

End of rally.

2nd rally
- A: flat serve
- B: crosscourt volley
- A: defensive boast
- B: drop shot
- A: lob (crosscourt)

End of rally.

3rd rally
- A: serve to middle
- B: drive
- A: volley (long)
- B: boast
- A: drop shot

End of rally.

4th rally
- A: backhand serve from right
- B: volley (straight)
- A: boast from back
- B: drop shot
- A: drop shot
- B: hard drive from front

End of rally.

5th rally
- A: flat serve from left
- B: volley (straight)
- A: volley boast
- B: lob (straight)

After this the rally is spontaneous.

Important Devise the rallies according to the abilities of the players, making rally sequences more difficult as players improve and progress.

Training in threes and fours

Squash can be played with more than two players on court. There are many advantages to this type of multiple-player training

- Better use of training time
- Everyone can be included
- Concentrated learning
- Many variations possible
  – introducing a more competitive element
  – involving 3-4 players
  – varying training intensity
  – altering training effort
- Provides demanding training

Important In every exercise there should be frequent movement within the group, i.e. after 2 minutes all parties should swap players.

Exercises for three players

Standard

- A plays a drive (straight)
- B and C play boasts

After every shot B and C must return to the T.

Variations

- A plays a drive (straight)
- B and C play volley boasts

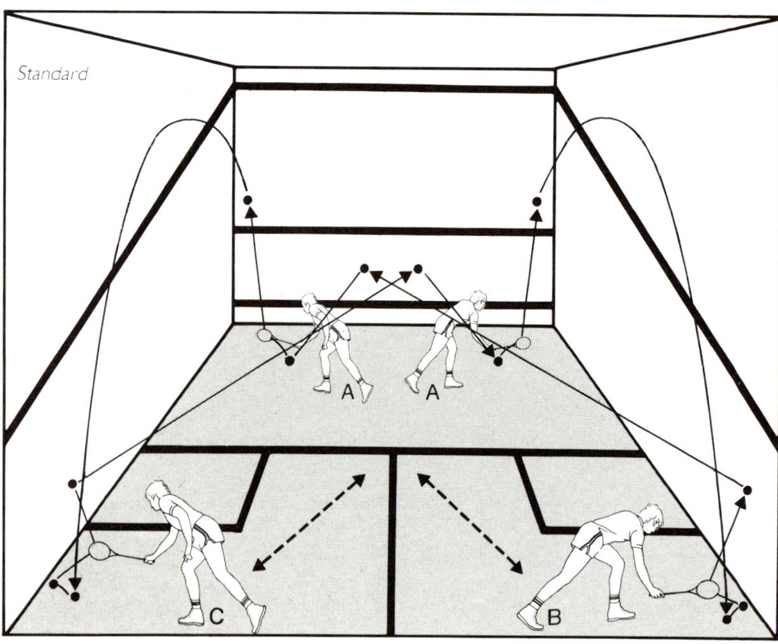

2 : 1

One player practises on one side with two players on the other.

After 3 minutes change players.

On the side where there are two players the following combinations can be practised:

- Back player: drop shot from the back
  Front player: straight drive
- Back player: straight drive
  Front player: volley

Drive – boast – drive

- A plays a drive from the front
- B plays a drive from the back
- C plays a boast from the back
- Repeat the sequence.

All players run to the T after each shot.

Variations

- C may also play a volley boast
- B may also play a drop shot from the back, then C plays a trickle boast.

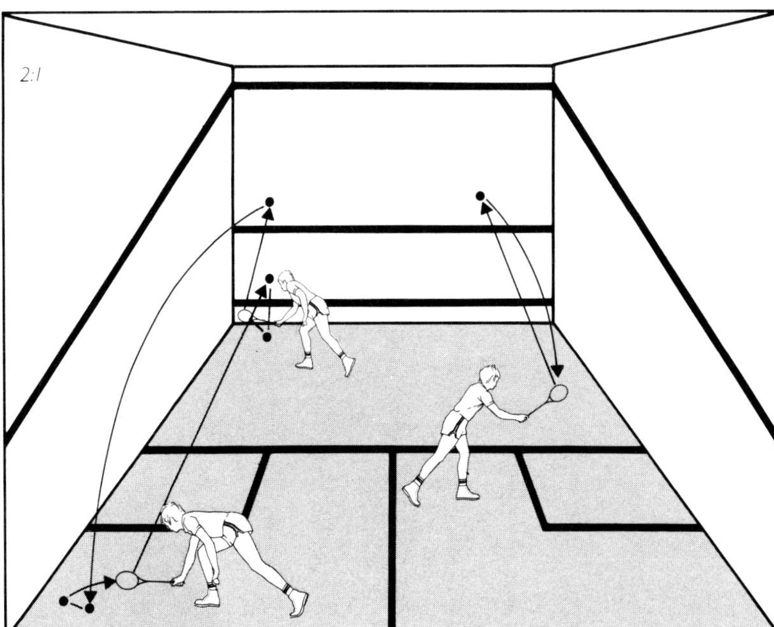

Boast – drop shot – drive
- A plays a boast
- B plays a drop shot from the back
- C plays a straight drive
- The sequence begins again.

Important
- Player A changes sides after the shot
- Player B stays at the front
- Player C must run to the T after the shot.

Boast – lob – volley
- A plays a boast
- B plays a lob (crosscourt)
- C plays a volley (straight)

Exercises for four players

Circling
Each player
- hits a 45° drive
- runs to the opposite back corner
- runs forwards to the front corner and then back to the T.

Variations
- Each player plays 2 or 3 strokes
- Use various stroke techniques (e.g. drive volley).

The following three exercises are appropriate only for the higher-ability players.

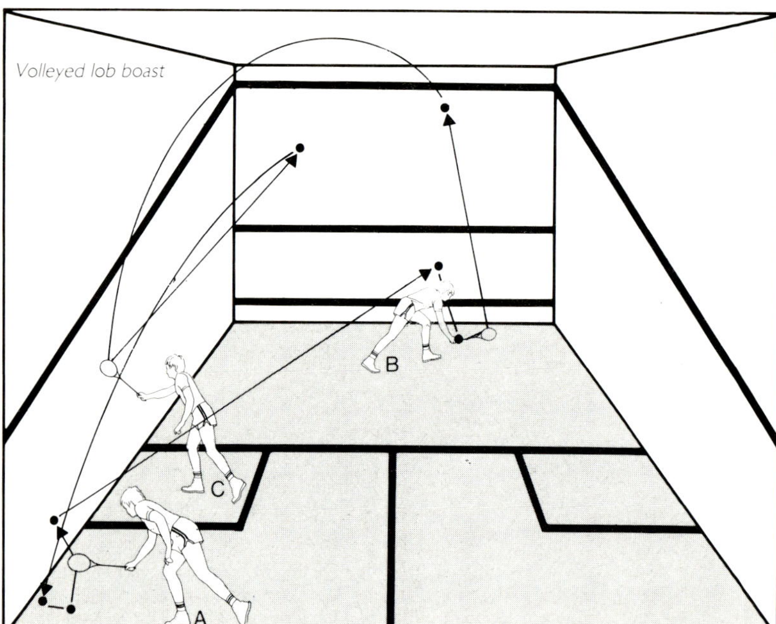

Volleyed lob boast

Tandem

Two players on each side of the court.

Mixed 1

- A plays a drive (straight)
- B plays a drive (straight) using 45° technique
- C plays a boast
- D plays a trickle boast
- The sequence begins again.

Mixed 2

- A plays a drive (crosscourt)
- B plays a defensive boast
- A plays a trickle boast
- C plays a drop shot from the front
- D plays a trickle boast
- The sequence begins again.

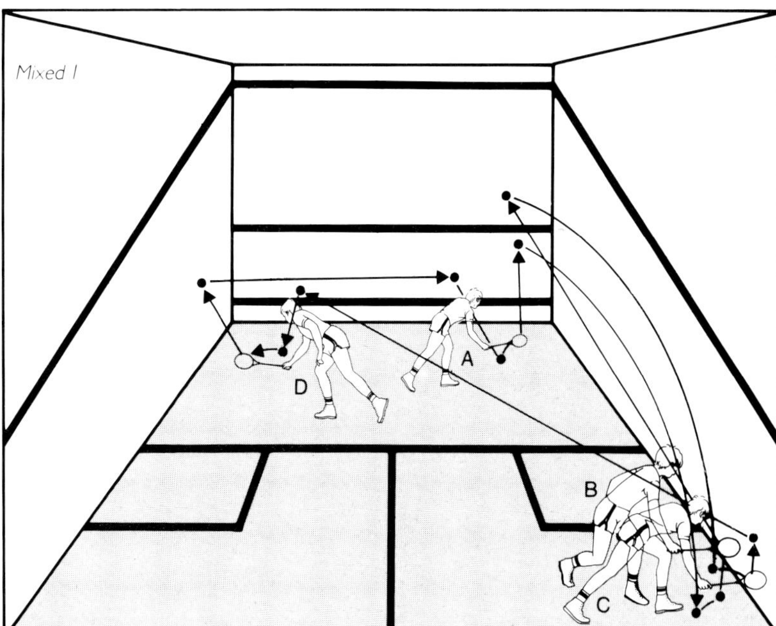

Physical training

It isn't only competitive players who need to have a high degree of speed, agility, strength and stamina. Gymnastics and fitness exercises help improve all these, but, done regularly, are also good for maintaining and improving your general fitness. Gymnastic exercises help strengthen your muscles and make your joints supple. You should do them in the following order:

- Loosening up
- Stretching
- Strengthening
- Stretching

Important Every muscle has its counterpart which permits movement in the opposite direction (bender-stretcher). To avoid one-sided loading always exercise one muscle, then the other. Gymnastic routines should exercise as many parts of the body as possible:
E.g. Lower thigh – upper thigh – back – stomach – shoulder – girdle – arms.
There is a wealth of exercises available for this purpose.
The photographs illustrate some of those particularly suitable for squash players.
Coaches and trainers are recommended to have specialist exercise books.

Strength exercises

In squash it isn't the level of maximum strength that is decisive. Particular demands are made on your resilience which can be improved with these exercises:

- Astride jumps with additional weights (bars, lead vest).
- Medicine ball exercises.
- Sit ups.
- Twisting exercises with small dumb-bells (2-5lb/1-2kg).

The following are good for resilience training:

- High speed movement.
- 4-6 series with about 10 repetitions.
- Breaks of about 3 minutes.

Stamina exercises

The best exercises for squash are interval movement sequences, which come closest to actual play, but basic stamina must also be improved and this can be done with the following exercises. The purpose of these is to attune and improve your cardio-circulatory system.

- Long distance running (up to 30 minutes) at a constant speed.
- Cross-country running across varied terrain.
- Interval running: 30-60 seconds at medium speed followed by 30-60 seconds slow trotting; 10-20 repetitions. Pulse rate should be 150 beats a minute after exertion.
- All lengthy squash exercises.

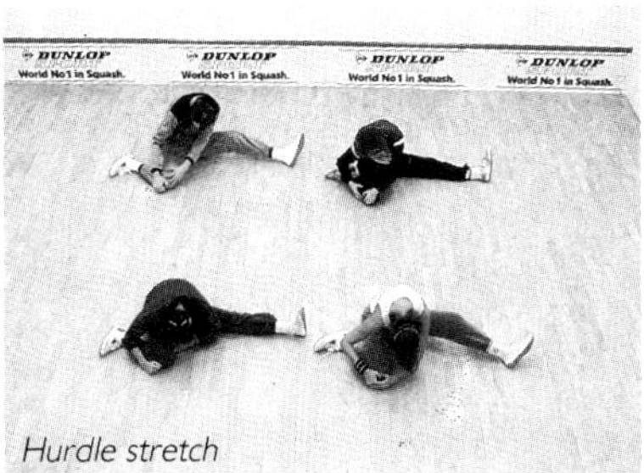

Hurdle stretch

Alternate lunges

Sit-ups

Sideways torso stretch

Forward torso stretch

Backward torso stretch

Speed exercises

- 20-30 yard/metre sprints
- Reaction exercises, particularly to visual stimuli
- Speed exercises on court.

The purpose of these is to improve your nerve-muscle system, co-ordination and reactions.

Agility exercises

These help extend your range of movement.

- All stretching exercises (preferably exercising the spine and shoulder girdle).

Circuit training

Circuit training is excellent for establishing and improving your general physical fitness. Circuit training can be done on court, but it's better to do it in a gymnasium.

Advantages

- Easy to carry out
- Degree and length of exertion can be tailored to individuals
- Specific improvement in strength, stamina and speed as required by the demands of squash
- Test results can be immediately assessed
- New exercises can always be introduced
- Many people are occupied at once.

Organisation

- Set up 6-8 stations each occupied by 2 players.
- While one is doing the exercise within a given time limit the other evaluates the results.
- 1 point is given for every exercise completed within the time limit.
- When all stations have been visited add up the total score. The higher the score the greater the fitness level.

Important You should take your pulse after each circuit. Don't begin the next circuit until it has gone down to 120-130 beats a minute.

Warming-up

Once again we would like to recommend that a pre-match warm up is essential.

- Warm up on court, or in the changing room or in a corner of the building
- Warm up for about 5 minutes.

Doing so lessens the chances of you hurting yourself, especially straining a muscle, and prepares your body for the game and puts you in the right frame of mind for playing.

Remember that if you don't warm up you will greatly increase the risk of injury.

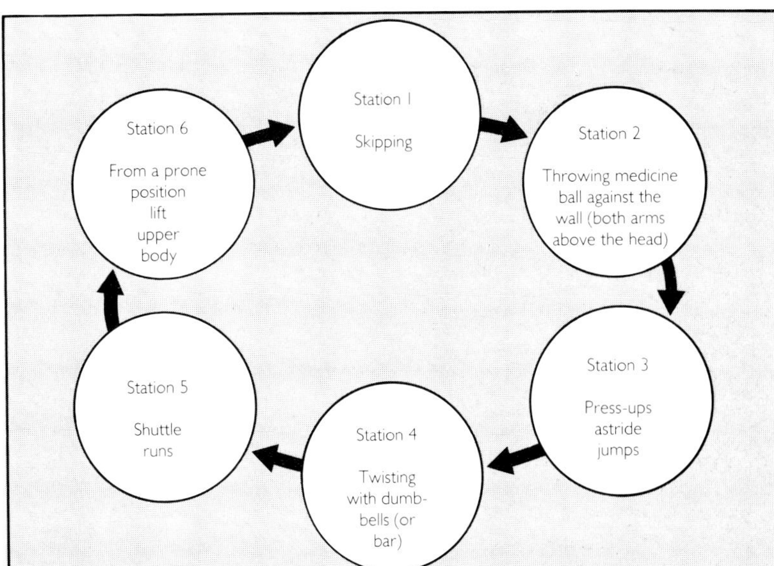

Competitions

The enormous range of squash competitions, games and tournaments guarantees that every player – regardless of how good – can gain a lot of pleasure from the game. This may involve, for instance, a good player giving a weaker opponent a few points starter and arranging for team matches to take account of the abilities of the players.

To ensure that a tournament or team match is a success you will certainly need to make sure beforehand that

- the venue provides good playing conditions
- participants are invited to play well in advance
- teams are matched in strength
- the type of the competition is appropriate for the motivation of the participants

Important tips for match play

- Play in a calm and concentrated way.
- Reduce any nervousness and exaggerated stress. Remember that it is only a game!
- Don't change your tactics.

Vary the rules

The rules can be adapted to the particular requirements of players, e.g.

- Shorten or lengthen the game
- Allow both server and returner to score points

Play with handicaps

- Give weaker players a head start of points.
- Don't allow better players to play certain strokes.

Novelty matches or tournaments

Novelty matches can be a lot of fun, especially in tournament form, and enable anybody to take part. Try

- playing with the wrong hand.
- playing with a balloon attached to your racket.
- playing with two against the club champion.

Try devising games which feature elements of squash in them.

Informal competitions

More casual players needn't adhere so strictly to the rules and systems that apply in serious competitive squash.

Singles tournaments

Everybody against everybody else

This system offers the best way of comparing performance. That is why it is used for ranking lists and is well suited for family and household championships. However, when planning a tournament using this system you shouldn't forget to allow for the time it takes. The number of participants shouldn't be too large. The number of matches is calculated as follows:

$$M = \frac{(n-1)\,n}{2}$$

M = number of matches
n = number of players

	A	B	C	D	Position
A		1:2	0:2	2:1	3
B	2:1		1:2	2:0	2
C	2:0	2:1		2:1	1
D	1:2	0:2	1:2		4

Simple knock-out system

This system is uncomplicated and particularly useful if there are a large number of participants.

The principle is that if you lose you are out and the winner carries on to the next round.

The players are put into a draw with the best players positioned so that they don't meet each other too early.

For example, in a tournament of 16, the best players will be allocated positions 1, 8, 9, and 16. If the list isn't fully occupied these players are give a bye. If there are too many players qualifying matches will need to be played to reduce the number to 16.

Simple knock-out system with consolation round

This is as for a simple knock-out system with the losers of the first round playing an additional consolation round, also under the knock-out system. This means that everyone taking part plays at least two games.

Simple knock-out system with consolation round and super consolation round

This is as for a simple knock-out system with consolation round but all those who lose in the second round play a further super consolation round.

Double knock-out system

In this system a player isn't out until after losing twice. This means it is possible for a player who loses in the first round still to win the tournament. To do so they will have to win the losers' round and then beat the winner of the winners' round twice.

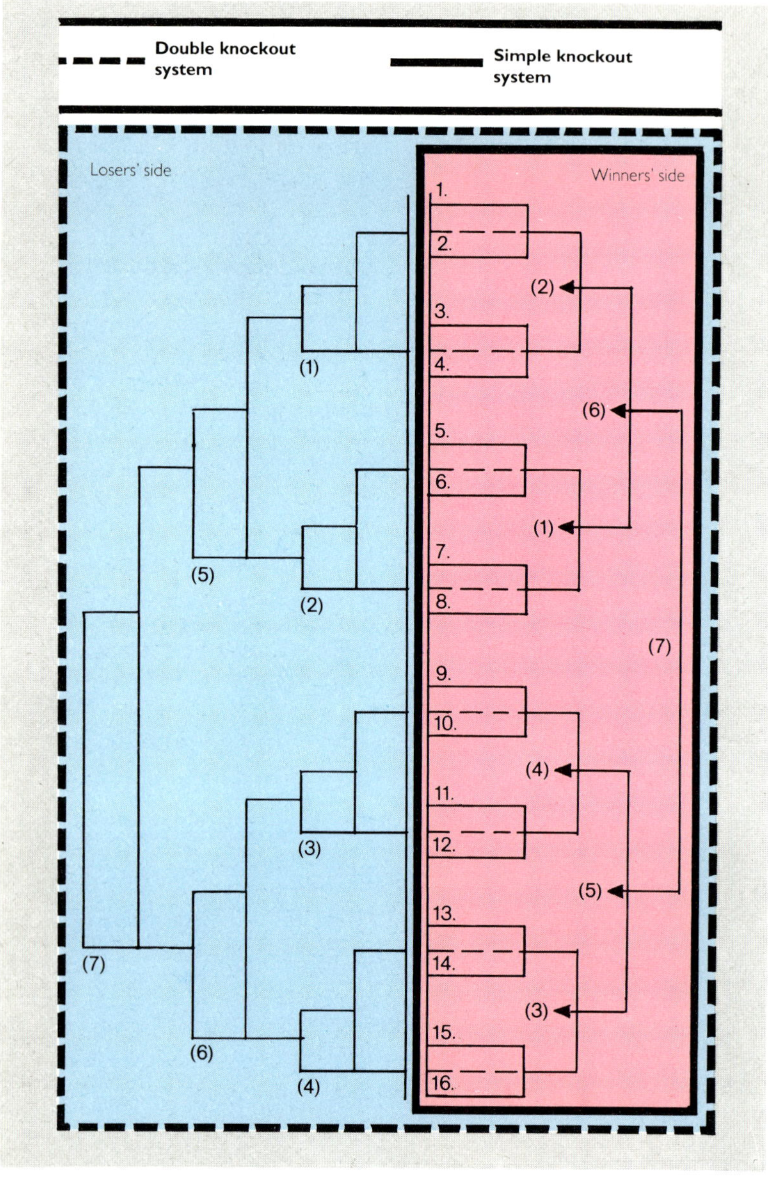
Double knockout system
Simple knockout system
Losers' side
Winners' side
1.
2.
3.
4.
5.
6.
7.
8.
9.
10.
11.
12.
13.
14.
15.
16.
(1)
(2)
(3)
(4)
(5)
(6)
(7)

Team competitions

Official

The number of players in a team competition is frequently the same at the local level as it is at the world team championships:

- 3 men
- 5 women (typical)

The players must be designated according to their ability on a scale of 1-5 (reserves are added to this total).

Order of play, men

3 player v 3 player
1 player v 1 player
2 player v 2 player

Order of play, women

5 player v 5 player
4 player v 4 player
1 player v 1 player
2 player v 2 player
3 player v 3 player
All matches are the best of three games.

Unofficial team competitions

There are two useful systems for these kind of competitions.

Teams of three

Each team consists of three players, who all play each other.

Cross-pairs system

A team consists of 4 or 6 players. A total of 8 or 12 singles matches are played. Individuals compete against each other in pairs, each crossing over to play the other opponent in his pair.

Emperor game

You will need 3, 4 or 5 courts. After 10 minutes play or one game

- the losers move to the court on the right
- the winners move to the court on the left
- the winner in the court on the extreme left stays there!

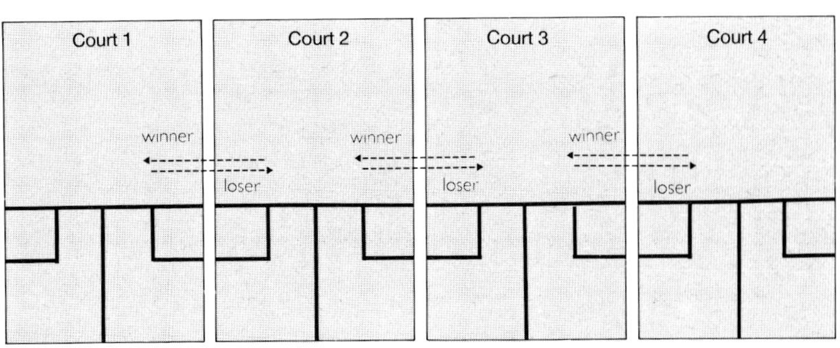

Theory

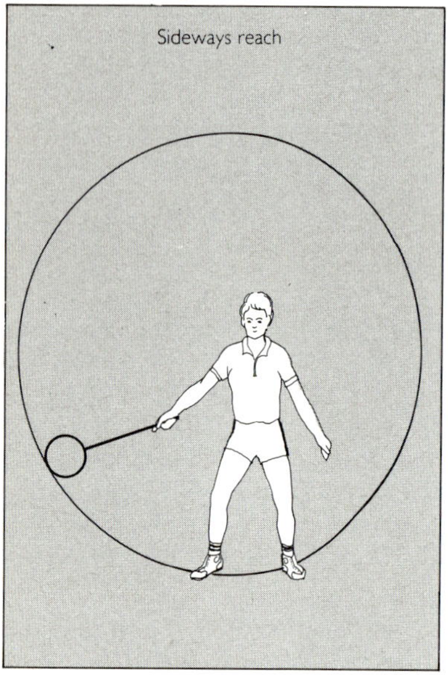

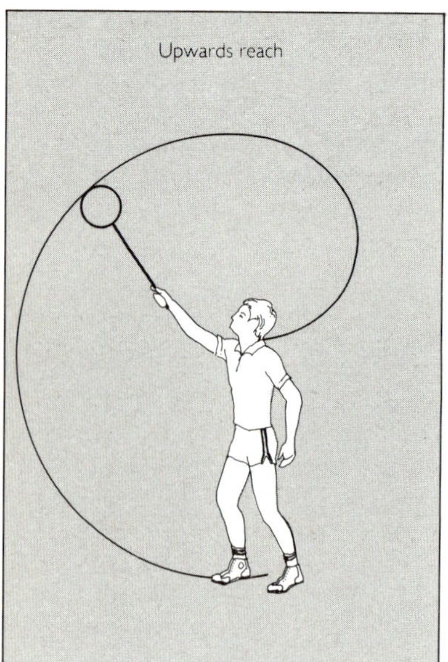

If you have a grasp of the theoretical side of squash it will help you

- Understand technical and tactical problems
- Recognise and resolve practical problems
- Speed up learning.

Reach

To play effectively, making the most of your full reach is crucially important.

Advantages

- cuts down running required
- improves opportunities for playing shots
- provides opportunities for playing a greater range of shots
- gives control of the T.

Extent

A 5ft 9in/1.75m tall player standing upright has a reach, with the racket

- upwards of about 8ft 9in to 9ft 3in/2.7 to 2.8m
- to the side of about 3ft 9in to 4ft 3in/1.15 to 1.3m
- forwards of 4ft/1.2m.

This means you can cover about half the width of the court and a considerable amount of space in front and behind you from one place.

Areas of impact

Reach is closely allied with where in space, and in relation to your own body, you actually hit the ball. Squash

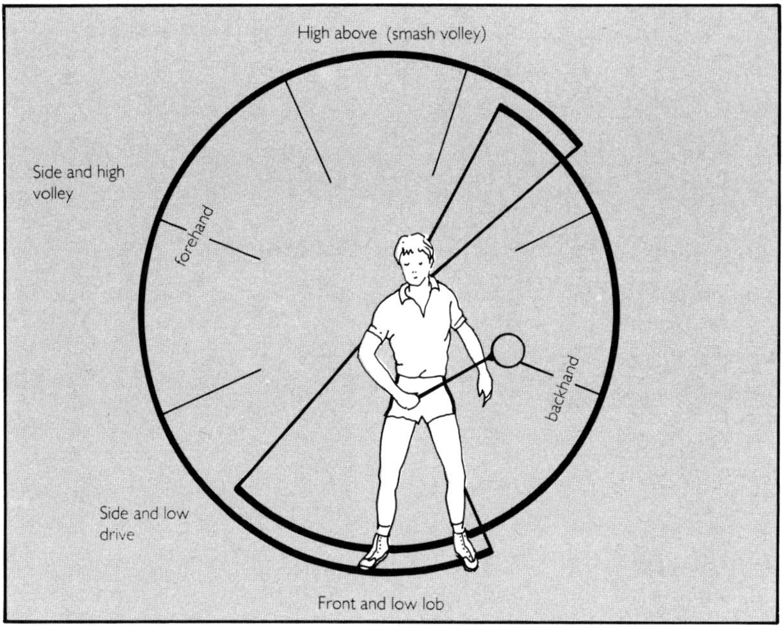

strokes are limited by the height of the tin. And as the ball can be played on the volley as well as after its first bounce, the main areas where the ball is hit are:

Front and low (lob)

The point is below the wrist level of the racket hand.

Side and low (drive)

The point of impact is to the side and low alongside the body at about the height of the racket hand.

Side and above (volley)

The point of impact is above and alongside the body at about head height or a little above.

High above (volley smash)

Impact on the ball is high above the head.

Important The reach sideways is different on the forehand from that on the backhand (see illustration).

Ball's flight

As well as being familiar with the different areas in relation to your own body that you hit the ball, you need to know about its behaviour in flight to have a good grasp of the precise result of different strokes.

High-long to back wall

Target area
close to the back wall.

Aims
to force your opponent from a good T position to the back;
to force your opponent to play a defensive return.

Strokes
lob, drive from the front.

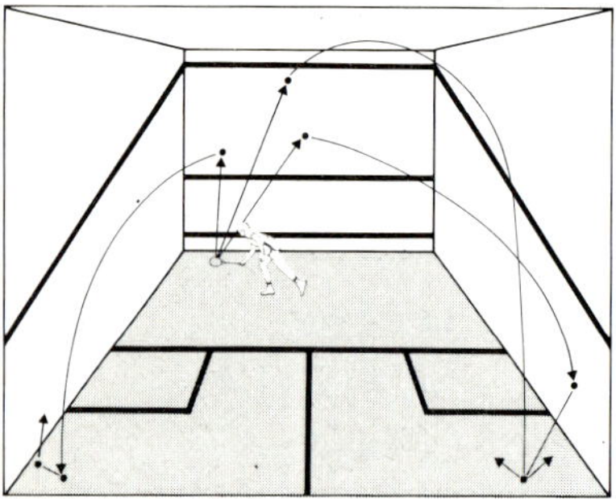

High-long to front wall

Target areas
high up on the front wall;
in the middle of the front wall at the height of the service line.

Aim
to keep the game open from a tight position.

Stroke
back corner defensive boast.

To differentiate more clearly between different types of long flat flight they will be divided into long-long and long-short, which refer to the length of the trajectory on to the front wall and the length of the ball after bouncing off the front wall.

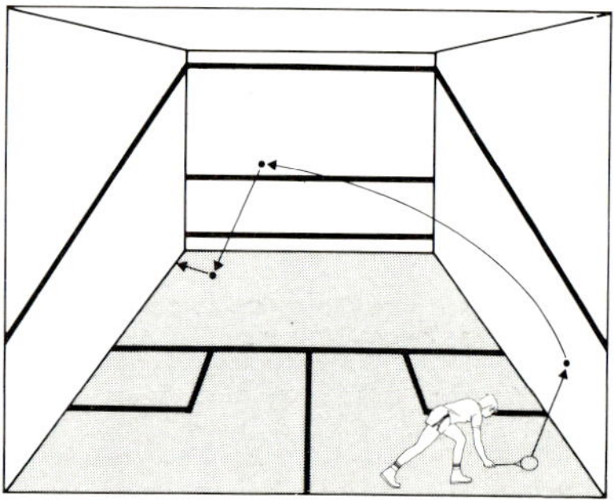

Flat and long-long

Target area
centre of court to the back wall.

Aims
to force your opponent into a defensive shot;
to score an outright winner.

Stroke
hard drive (straight or crosscourt).

Important To make an outright winner the ball will need to make its second bounce early.

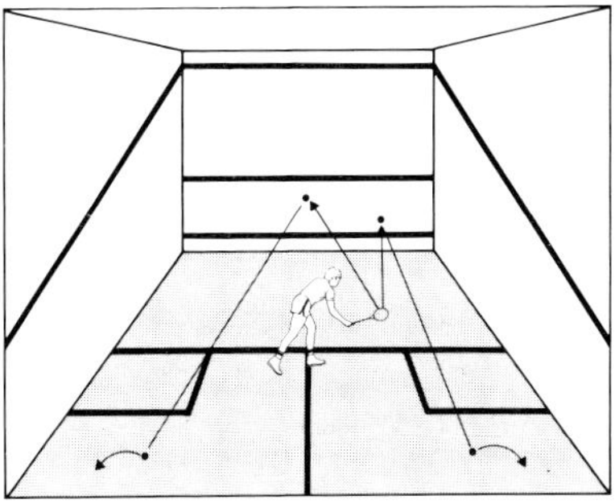

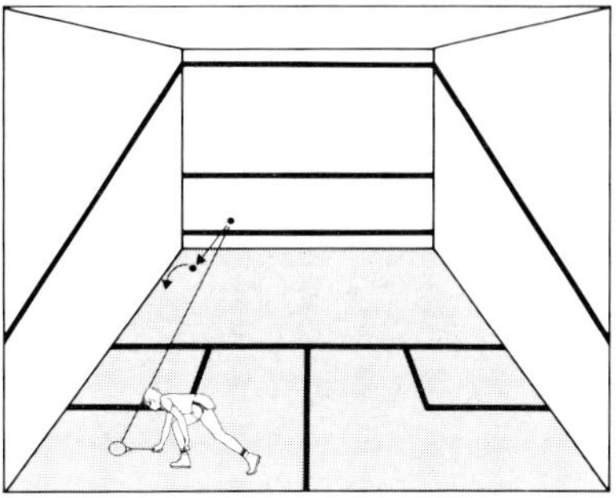

Flat and long-short

Target area
close to the tin.

Aims
to force your opponent forwards from a good T position;
to score an outright winner.

Stroke
drop shot from the back.

Flat, short

Target area
close to the tin.

Aims
to force your opponent forwards from a good T position;
to score an outright winner.

Strokes
drop shot from the front, trickle boast, short volley boast, etc.

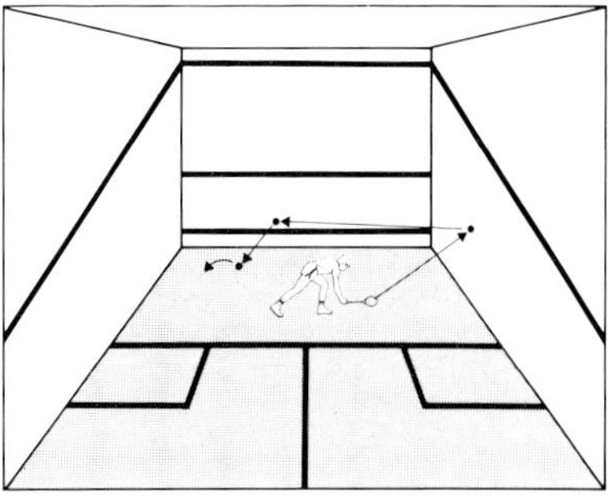

Ball speed

It is interesting that in tennis, table tennis and squash initial ball speeds immediately after impact are roughly the same. However, the loss of ball speed is lowest in squash.

In squash the ball speed varies between 12 and 120mph (20 and 200km/h). The type of stroke played determines the ball speed: when the ball is hit forcefully it travels faster and when it is pushed it obviously moves more slowly.

Important It is easy to be mistaken about the apparent speed of a squash ball. For example, when a player makes a fast drop shot from the back the speed on the ball is less than you imagine as a great deal of the effort on the shot is converted into spin on the ball.

Ball speeds

Speed mph (km/h)	**Stroke**
slow 12-35 (20-60)	all strokes with a lot of backspin
medium 35-60 (60-100)	all strokes with normal backspin
fast 60-120 (100-200)	all strokes without or with only a little spin, but performed fast

This table of ball speeds refers to their initial speed immediately after being hit. Obviously, the speed drops considerably as the ball travels through the air, mainly because of air resistance.

In spite of this loss of speed, squash is one of the fastest ball games in the world.

Stroke-action speed

Your racket arm can reach a maximum speed of about 30mph (50km/h), measured at the centre of your hand; and a racket can travel at speeds of up to 60mph (100km/h), measured at the centre of the racket face.

Contact between ball and racket

The ball is in contact with the racket for an extremely short time; about 1/250th second. During this brief contact time the ball, depending on the strength of the shot, is carried between 3/8 and 2inches (10 and 50mm). On shots with a slow action the ball is taken only 3/8 to 1 inch (10 and 25mm) and on fast shots 1 to 2inches (25 to 50mm). The relatively long contact on hard-hit shots is understandable when you consider that the harder the ball is hit the more it loses its shape.

Reaction time

It takes a very small, but measurable, length of time for us to react to a given stimulus – in squash, to the ball's approach – and so to move or respond appropriately. This is our reaction time: the time it takes to respond to a signal. The average reaction time for a simple response is

- to sights 0.18 seconds
- to sounds 0.14 seconds

As squash isn't a matter of simple reactions but of complex ones, often calling for a choice between several alternatives, your reaction time will include the time you take making your choice.

For example, should you play a forehand or backhand? Clearly, making this decision prolongs your reaction time.

With this in mind, and given that in squash it is mainly visual stimuli we respond to, we can assume that a standard reaction time for average players is about 0.25 second. With practice and talent you can reduce this reaction time to the 0.18 second average for a simple reaction. Top-level players all have, and need to have, high-speed responses.

Spin

In tennis and table tennis you can, with the right technique, give the ball
- topspin
- backspin
- sidespin
- no spin

In squash, with a few exceptions such as the volley smash, the strokes used give the ball a moderate to extreme backspin only. As the ball is struck full and level with the racket on the volley smash it has no spin at all.

All other squash strokes give the ball backspin. With spin a ball can achieve a maximum of about 150 revolutions a second immediately after being hit. This is possible on strokes with extremely strong backspin.

On a shot played with backspin the ball's flight is longer than on a shot hit equally hard but without spin.

The reason for this is that the backward turning ball heats an airstream which keeps it in the air longer.

Assuming equal effort on the shot, the greater the spin on the ball the slower it will be.

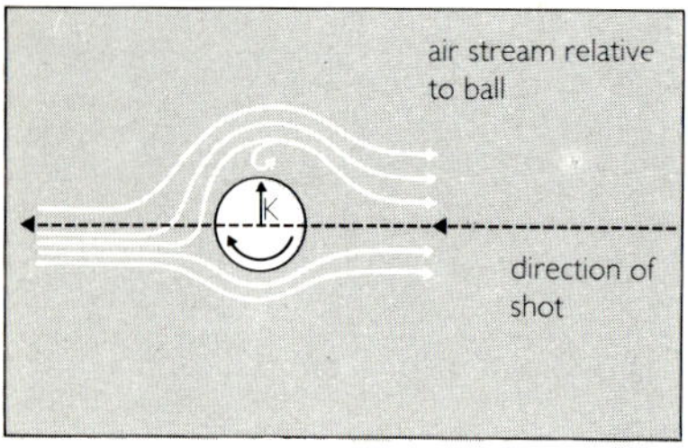

Anticipation

You might well think that squash can't actually be played the way it is meant to be, given that
- The ball reaches very high speeds (up to 125mph/200km/h).
- The ball is in contact with the racket for a very short time (1/250th second) and can only be carried for a maximum of 2inches/50mm during this time.
- The spin on the ball is extremely high (up to 150 revolutions a second).
- Your reaction takes at least 0.18 second.
- The position of your racket on the ball must be exact.
- You need to take into account the flight path, spin and point of impact on the ball.

Clearly, in practice this isn't the case, of course. This is because we can plan actions in advance: we anticipate.

Essentials for anticipation

- Awareness of the flight path, speed and direction of the ball
- Experience of the effects of spin on the ball, how the racket needs to be held, how an opponent moves,

and above all how the ball played to an opponent is most likely to be returned

We can safely state the following:

- The better your anticipation and the more experience you have the better your squash will be.
- These abilities can be acquired through training and match play.
- Your trainer will play a major role in this training process.
- Ultimately, the limiting factor is yourself.

Dynamics of squash

Here we look at what happens visibly when we make a series of movements, and what happens in our brains and bodies as we do so.

Run-up and making shots

Before your arm plays a stroke you go through the following phases:

Observation

By concentrating hard you should observe as much as possible. This includes:

- Position and movement of your opponent.
- Direction and length of the shot.
- Spin and ball speed.

Assessment

On the basis of what you see, you size up all the circumstances. Experience plays a major role in this: the more experienced you are the sounder your assessment will be.

Decision

After observing and assessing the situation you decide on the best course of action for the circumstances, and from the tactical choices available.

Action

The process of observation, assessment and decision leads to action, which is the outcome of the three previous phases.

All four phases overlap and are often partly automatic in experienced players. If a match-play situation doesn't allowed for planned response (for instance if you make a mistaken judgement of the oncoming ball) you will be able to react only with a reflex response.

Breakdown of actions

Actions are initiated by

- Preparedness for any given situation (for instance at the start of a game an opponent awaiting the serve or in a rally an opponent expecting a lob).
- The target (for example, to place the ball near the back wall) and the purpose of the action (to force an opponent to play a defensive return).
- A conscious personal decision (for example, 'I am going to serve').

Anticipation and response

Assessing actions

Your actions are continually monitored by receptors, or to put it more simply, feelers in your muscles, sinews and tendons. Your eyes also – as far as they can – control your actions. This control or feedback is then evaluated by the brain as success or failure.

Correcting actions

Being able to recognise a departure from a correct movement and that you have made a mistake means you can correct your errors. Often you can correct an error as you are carrying out an action, but as a rule you realise a mistake has been made only after playing the shot.

Important Always recognise a mistake when you make one, correct it and don't make it again in the same situation. Be aware of circumstances in which you tend to make mistakes.

Learning actions

The most important things you need for this are visual, written or verbal information. The more expert information you get from a trainer, a friend or helper the quicker you will learn.

The following sources of information are at a player's disposal.

Information visual	verbal
1. Demonstrations	1. Descriptions
2. Films (normal/slow motion)	2. Explanations
3. Videos	3. Instructions
4. Picture series (photos/illustrations)	
5. Photographs	
6. Illustrations	

Important When giving information it should be accurate, brief and precise.

Everyone should have someone who can tell them how they are playing. This should be a two-way process: you tell them where their strengths and weaknesses lay and they tell you yours. Give others tips and listen to theirs. Praise partners when it is called for and avoid destructive criticism, although positive suggestions are helpful and should be welcome.

Equipment and facilities

Rackets

The range of rackets on the market has increased considerably in recent years. Various types are available in the shops and it is worth knowing what differences the variations make.

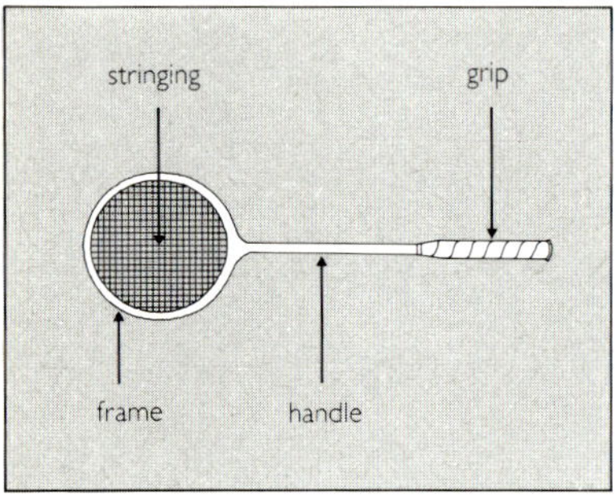

Frame

Frames are made of various materials
- wood
- synthetics
- metal

Combinations of these materials are also possible. The maximum size of the racket head is specified, and there are two sizes on the market:
- normal head
- medium head

Grip

Unlike badminton and tennis rackets there are no differences in the widths of squash racket handles.

Important The grip should be wrapped in leather or terry towelling.

Stringing

The stringing can either be synthetic or gut. With cheaper rackets the stringing is provided by the manufacturer and is almost always synthetic.

Buying rackets

- Don't buy the cheapest racket, which can be a false economy.
- Get advice from experienced players or your trainer first.
- Have a good racket strung by the dealer when you buy it.
- The dearest rackets aren't always the best.

Beginners

Choose a medium-priced racket that costs between £20 and £40 and make sure it is one with synthetic stringing.

Advanced players

Individually strung rackets with a frame to match will improve your game. Players who hit the ball hard should use hard-strung squash rackets, whereas delicate play is better achieved by using regular to soft stringing.

Various types of rackets, balls and other equipment

Experts

Expert players will invariably opt for gut stringing. It does wear out faster than synthetic stringing but has better qualities for squash as it is more elastic and provides players with greater feel and control.

Looking after your racket

- Replace terry towelling grips when they no longer absorb sweat.
- Consider covering leather grips with self-adhesive tape.
- Buy a racket cover to protect the stringing.
- Damaged strings can be repaired: don't have the entire stringing replaced immediately.
- If the grip is too smooth it can be made more slip resistant by roughening it or using grip powder.
- Don't expose your rackets to direct sunlight.

Balls

There are four types of ball available

- Blue dot ball (very fast)
- Red dot ball (fast)
- White dot ball (slow)
- Yellow dot ball (very slow)

Some firms no longer produce white dot balls and generally players at different levels should use the different types of ball as follows

Beginners = blue dot ball

Advanced beginners = red dot ball

Competitive players = yellow dot ball.

The blue and red balls also have the advantage for beginners that, because of their bounciness, they don't always need to be warmed up by being struck very firmly.

Important The height of the ball's bounce and its speed are also affected by external temperature. The air inside the ball expands when warmed, altering these characteristics of the ball's behaviour.

The Court

The squash court has fixed dimensions.

The walls of squash courts are made of concrete combined with a special plaster, and the floor is made of semi-vaulted parquet. Lighting levels should be at least 450 watts.

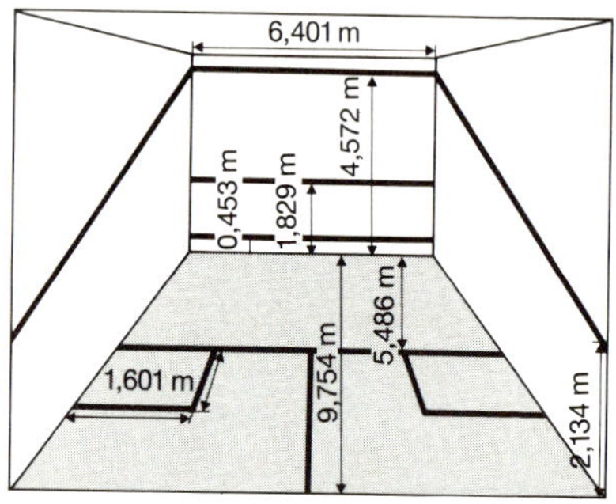

Court dimensions

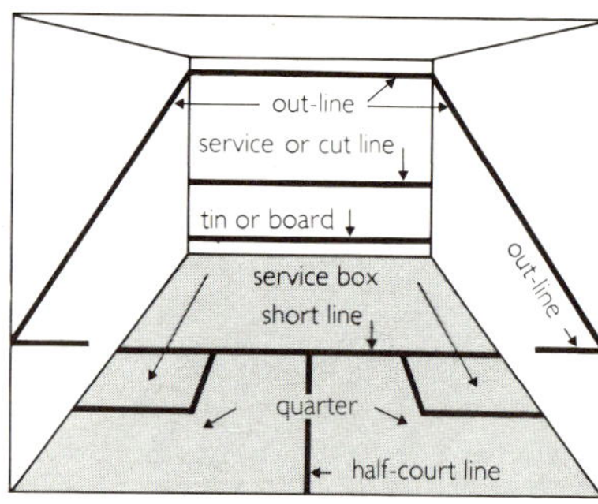

Court areas and lines

Important The prescribed dimensions and features of the court means playing conditions and environment are standard.

Dress

Obviously, you can play squash in any sports clothing you wish. The ISRF (International Squash Rackets Federation) prescribes white or pastel dress for competitions as these colours provide the best contrast to the ball.

Tracksuit

This is an essential part of sports clothing. Don't remove it until you start sweating.

Top

Choose an absorbent material and a comfortable size and cut.

Shorts or skirts

These should allow you plenty of freedom of movement.

Shoes

You can manage with ordinary gym shoes but special squash shoes do have advantages

- The slip resistant sole, designed for parquet, provides a very secure grip.
- The rounded casings protect against sprains.

Socks

You should only wear socks made of a hard wearing absorbent material.

Sweat and head bands

There aren't just a fashionable fad but are extremely useful and to be re-commended.

Rules

The following is a shortened version of the most important rules in accordance with the regulations laid down by the International Squash Rackets Federation (ISRF).

Scoring

- According to the decision of the tournament organiser, a match can be won in two or three games.
- A game is played up to nine points.
- The first player to score 9 points wins the game, except if the score is 8:8 when the receiver may choose before the serve is played, to extend the game to 10 points or end it at 9 as normal. The receiver must make this decision clear to the referee and the server.

Scoring points and winning the ball

- Only the server can score (as in volleyball and badminton).
- A receiver who takes the point wins the serve but doesn't score.

Play

Service

Players toss for the serve before the start of play.

Each player chooses a side of the racket. The racket is then spun and the player whose side is uppermost wins.

- The server continues to serve until losing a rally.
- At the start of a game and each time on winning the serve a player may choose which side to serve from.
- After winning a point the server must serve from the other side and continue to alternate while remaining server or until the end of a game. After a service error which isn't returned or a rally which ends with a let the server must serve from the same side again.
- If the serve is played from the wrong side there is no penalty and the serve is good unless the receiver makes no attempt to return the shot and demands that the serve is played from the correct side.
- When serving, the ball must be dropped or thrown into the air without touching the wall or floor before it is struck.
- The ball must be played straight onto the front wall between the service line and the out line in such a way that after bouncing off the wall it lands in the opposite back quarter of the court from where the server served from, unless it is intercepted by the receiver before landing (volley).
- A server who makes no attempt to play the ball after having dropped or thrown it up may serve again without penalty.
- The server must keep at least one foot in the service box while serving without it touching the line.

- There is a fault on the serve if
  – the player commits a foot fault (foot on the line),
  – the ball lands on or under the service line,
  – after the serve the ball lands on or in front of the short line, on the half court line or outside the correct quarter.
- The receiver can accept a bad serve. In this case it becomes good.
- The server loses the rally and so the serve if he makes two consecutive service faults. This doesn't apply if
- the serve is accepted,
- the exchange ends in a let.
  – the ball hits a wall or the floor before being hit, or if it isn't hit at all or is hit twice.
  – the ball is hit on or under the tin or out.
  – the ball touches the server's person, clothing or equipment before its second bounce or before the receiver has played it.

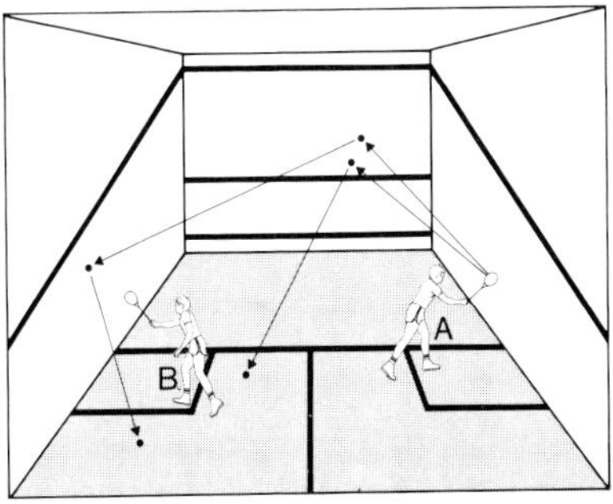

Good serve
A hits the ball above the service line into B's quarter. Both possible flights of the ball are illustrated in the drawing above. Note the position of the server's feet.

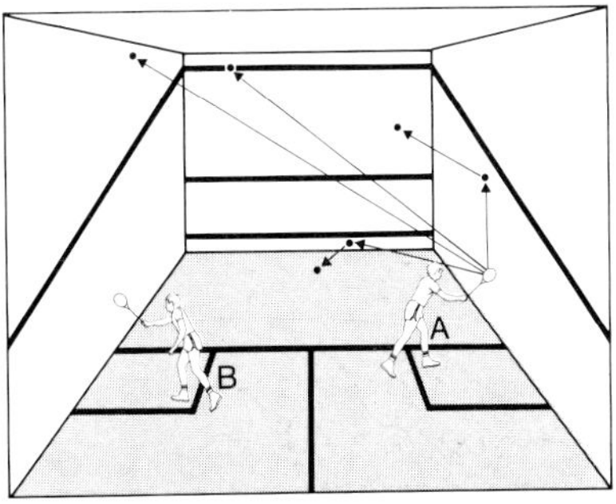

Bad serve
A loses the serve immediately because the ball goes out of play (1), touches the red out-line (2), hits the tin (3) or isn't played directly onto the front wall (4).

Good stroke

A stroke is good if the player hits the ball onto the front wall above the tin before it has bounced twice. The stroke isn't good if the ball is struck twice or hit out of court.

Let

The ball mustn't be played if it endangers an opponent. Such situations are dealt with in the following let rules.
A let may be given if
– because of the player's position, he could not avoid hitting his opponent with the ball
– ball hits an object on court
– the player declines to hit the ball to avoid injuring an opponent
– a player touches an opponent while playing the shot.
A let must be given if
– the receiver isn't ready to play
– the ball is damaged during play.
After a let a rally is played again. The serve or rally that ends in a let doesn't count and the server serves again from the same service box.
No let should be given if a player (even if all the other conditions for a let are met) attempts to play the ball.
If there is no appeal from either player then, in principle, a let should not be given.

Hitting an opponent with the ball

If on an otherwise good shot the ball hits an opponent's person, clothing or equipment before it hits the front wall the striker wins the rally if the ball,.hit correctly, would have hit the front wall without touching another wall first.

Examples of a let

Let? Yes!

You can ask for a shot to be taken again when the players are in various positions. In the case illustrated here A has no chance of hitting the ball unless B makes room. It should always be possible to play a shot without the risk of injuring your opponent with your racket. You ask for a let and the serve is played again.

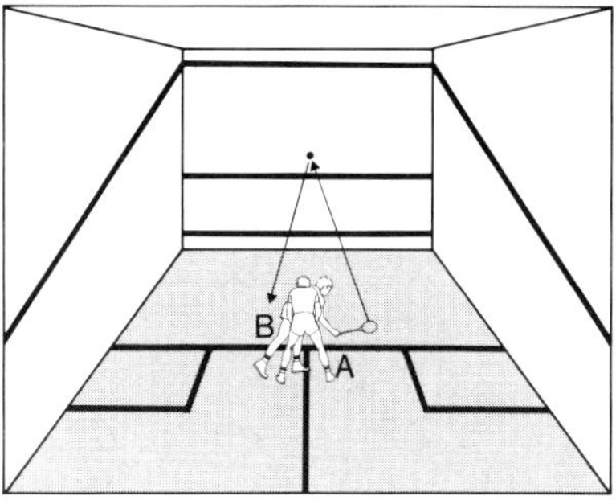

Let? No!

As the illustration shows, it can happen that your opponent (B) runs directly into the path of the ball which would have hit the front wall first. In this case A wins the point.

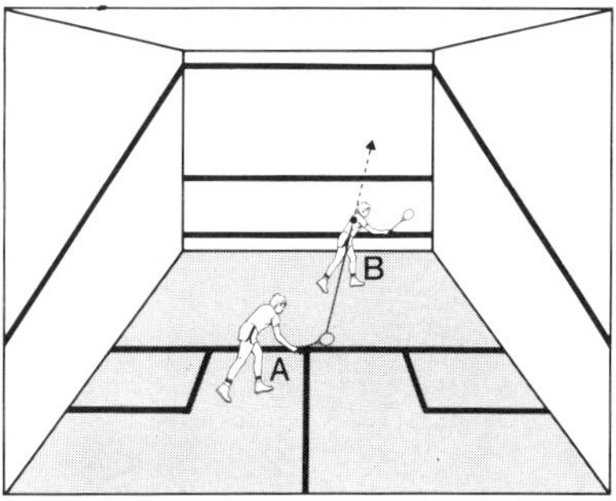

Let? Yes!

A hits the ball against the right side wall. B is standing in the way and comes into contact with the ball. If the ball had been on a direct path to the front wall A would have won the point. In this instance the trajectory of the ball is off a side wall before hitting the front wall. In this example, once contact is made with the ball the serve will be repeated.

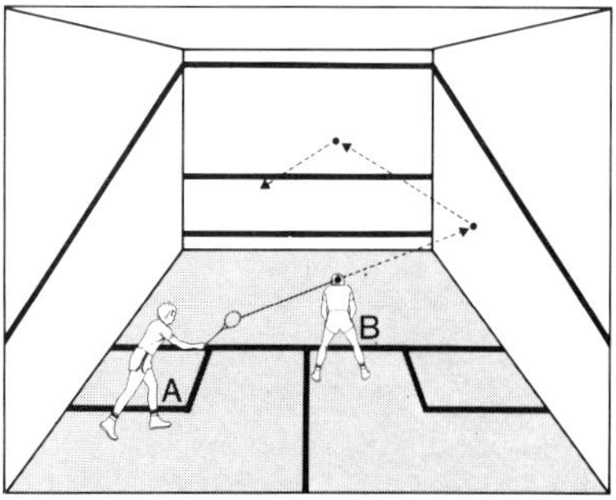

Adequate sight and room to play the ball and interference

- After a shot players must make every effort to give way to their opponent. In particular:
  – The player must make every effort to allow the opponent to see the ball so that it can be returned.
  – The player must make every effort, in as far as position permits, to give the opponent the opportunity to play a shot directly on to the front wall or on to a side wall near the front wall.
- In the event of interference the referee will, on appeal or on his or her own initiative, award the ball to the opponent if convinced that the player did not make every effort to avoid the interference.
- If, however, the referee believes that the player did make every effort to avoid the interference, a let can be awarded.
- In the event of unnecessary physical contact by either player the referee can interrupt play and award the point accordingly.

Warm-up

The referee will allow the players a maximum five minutes warm-up on court together immediately before the start of play.

Interrupting play

- Only the referee may interrupt play (not the players).
- Between each game there is a break of 1 minute and between the fourth and fifth games a 2-minute break. The players may leave the court during these breaks.

The marker and the referee

Usually a match is officiated by a referee assisted by a marker, but one person may carry out both duties. When referees make a decision they tell the players; the marker repeats it and gives the score.

Rules and fair play

- Any club player will be pleased to explain further rules to you.
- At the recreational level of play, every player should be willing to play fair and, in case of doubt, offer their partner a let.